ECHOES

Gerard Casey

ECHOES

Τὸ μη δῦνόν ποτε πῶς ἄν τις λάθοι;

Heraclitus, Bywater XXVII

SOPHIA PERENNIS

HILLSDALE NY

Third edition, 2005
© Sophia Perennis
Second edition, Phudd Bottom Press, 1999
First edition, Rigby & Lewis, 1990
Foreword © Charles Lock, 1990
Introduction to 'South Wales Echo' © David Blamires, 1973
Frontispiece and cover drawing © Timothy Hyman

For information, address:
Sophia Perennis, P.O. Box 611
Hillsdale NY 12529
sophiaperennis.com

Library of Congress Cataloging-in-Publication Data

Library of Congress Cataloging-in-Publication Data

Casey, Gerard.
Echoes / Gerard Casey.—3rd ed.

p. cm.

ISBN 1 59731 036 0 (pbk: alk. paper)
ISBN 1 59731 037 9 (hardback: alk. paper)
I. Title
PR6053.A796E27 2005
821'.7142—dc22   2005010338

For her dedication and help the Publishers are deeply grateful to Louise de Bruin,
and they wish to express especial regards and gratitude also to:
Richard Wilson, the late G. Wilson Knight, Frank Kibblewhite,
John Packham, Dennis O'Connor, Alan Harris, Doug Kite

The author gratefully acknowledges the debt he owes to the many poets whose works have
brought him their inspiration and contributed to the writing of *Echoes,* and draws
the reader's attention to the recently-published volume of letters and essays entitled
Night Horizons (1997) also published by Phudd Bottom Press.

Acknowledgments are due to:

Jonathan Cape Ltd. for permission to print versions of poems by George Seferis.

The Anglo Welsh Review in which 'Easter Morning,' 'Anamnesis,' and 'The Eumenides' first appeared.

The Enitharmon Press, which first published 'South Wales Echo' and 'Between the Symplegades'.

Studies in Comparative Religion, which first printed 'The Shield of Achilles' and 'True Listening'.

Gerard Casey was born in South Wales in 1918.
After farming for many years in Kenya he returned to England and now lives in Dorset.

for Mary

'witness of all things is the spirit'

Arul

Contents

Foreword and Word on the Hearing of *Echoes*

In a culture that confers value on individualism, on the distinction and authenticity of voice and being, echo is a term of derogation. Connoting what is imitative, derivative, secondary, echo disowns originality. As a mythical figure — rather a voice than a figure — Echo survives as an ever-fading admonition, warning us not of the fate of unrequited love but of the course of love when there is confusion of identity, when the margins between self and other are wavering and indistinct. Our culture's received reading of the myths of Echo and Narcissus solicits concern for the distinct inwardness of our identity and the secure borders of our individuality.

When a poet names a sequence of his writings *Echoes* there may be a temptation to overlook the title, to see in it mere self-effacement, sheer littleness of claim. On the contrary, Gerard Casey's book of *Echoes* undoes what has been done with echoes: in place of the unoriginal and imitative, Casey gives to echo a poetic strength and a metaphysic. If echo disowns originality, disclaims the presence of being within voice, it does so the better to measure and negotiate distances. Recognizing that there are no original voices, because originality inheres only in the Word who is also a person, the voice who is also the creator, Casey makes of echo the very condition of the fallen cosmos.

Echo is not a mere negative, a perpetual symptom of loss: like a sign, an echo refers elsewhere. In this volume will be found allusions to Jakob Boehme, the mystic for whom all things bear the signature of the Maker, and for whom all signs are signatures. In heaven, the place of Divine Presence, there is no need of signs, for there is not that distance from presence that takes a signature. Echo is to language what sign is to things. If we have nothing but signs and echoes we may come to see all quest as repetition, and repetition as futility. But mystics such as Boehme, and the Kierkegaard of *Repetition*, have always understood, that which indicates loss and absence carries within it not just a trace or echo but the very presence of that which is absent . . . Once the Incarnation is properly comprehended, semiotics no longer fits into an abstract scheme of signs and referents. Because, through the Incarnation, matter partakes of the divine, and because all signs necessarily possess materiality, have existence in the real, not the ideal world, therefore all signs are sacraments.

Language, whether poetic or otherwise, is for most people more of a concept than a thing. In order that a neo-Platonic semiotics might be sustained, we are encouraged to see as arbitrary the dependence of writing on alphabets and ink, and the dependence of speech on ears and vocal chords. Language has retained the privileged status of Idea, even when we are otherwise so scientific as to allow the dependence of, for example, a tree on the materiality of wood. We see nothing arbitrary in the connection between a concept and the materiality of its being — except in language. That is at the very nub of *Echoes*, for the echo-effect is so strange, so ill-fitting to all our assumptions about language, that we are compelled to think of sound-waves, to seek explanation in acoustics. No other sound produced by the human voice so directs the hearer to acoustics rather than to semantic intentions. Echo as a phenomenon insists, with unparalleled success, on the materiality of voice — of voice, therefore, not as sign but as sacrament.

Taken not as a phenomenon but as a literary device, a rhetorical trope, echo can be a term for allusion or metalepsis or transumption. By this trope is meant something less exact, more suggestive than quotation. It was the very hubris of Romanticism to eschew allusion in the pursuit of originality. That it was a vain ambition is obvious to those who understand language to be not a concept but a historically-determined and much-used thing. It was precisely through such an understanding that Pound and Eliot could undo the Romantic inheritance by the revival of echo and allusion. It is, of all modern poets, David Jones, artist and engraver of alphabets and scripts, who has best understood the materials out of which and with which poetry is uttered and created. And David Jones, even more than Eliot, is the voice to resonate most clearly in Casey's major poem "South Wales Echo".

As a specific rhetorical term for echo, metalepsis has a curious, intermittent history (outlined by John Hollander in "Appendix: The Trope of Transumption", in *The Figure of Echo*, 1981). To cite, to copy, to come after — the negative connotations of echo — go together with translate, partake and participate of and in a prior instance. In order to deny the participatory force of echo it is often asserted that the echoes in *The Waste Land* are "ironic" — as if irony were the only alternative to reactionary nostalgia. In this fashion Eliot, Pound and Jones have all been grossly misread: for them echo affirms tradition not as mere linear continuance but as cumulation and partaking. It may be helpful to introduce the theological concept of *perichoresis* — with its constituents of flux, thoroughness, interpenetration, the allness of each and the eachness of all — in order to grasp the function of echo in the flux of language. Thus echo can be transformed from symptom of loss into the force of recuperation — always on the understanding that recuperation does not look backward but advances cumulatively.

Gerard Casey's echoes are made of allusions, quotations and translations. Lest we think a translation a derivative text, a substitute for an original, Casey arranges the volume so as to make plain the dependence of "originals" on other texts, the vanity of originality, and the status of all writing as echoing, all verse as version.

Fittingly, the first part, "Versions", is introduced in the way of an epigraph by a poem, "Voices", that is itself a translation. Far from being detached or separated, offering simplicity and entrance, this first poem is already complicit with the complexity that follows — that has already begun. Making use of the format of a book, the poems are arranged in pairs on facing pages, reflecting, mirroring, glossing each other, but turning also, gaining and losing in echo and translation, turning, versing, reversing and revising, that visions might be born of revisions. Each pair of poems presents the reader with doubleness, not self-contained as type and anti-type or original and copy but a doubleness that initiates a series: "initiates" is too loose, for there can be no poem without its pair, its unoriginal predecessor. And so we are moved, from a version of Shakespeare, seen afresh for the absence of the answer — "'Tis the god Hercules, whom Antony lov'd, Now leaves him" — to Cavafy's version, in which the missing line is reinstated as title.

So, between Cavafy and Herodotus, Elytis and Heraclitus, Homer and Sikelianos, the themes are repeated and returned, a dialogue of Greece with itself that is also a dialogue with and within the English language and modern civilization. The unity of classical civilization gives a linguistic continuity to the line of Greek poets from Hesiod to Elytis, even as that civilization is not confined to one language but gives itself, mythically, imaginatively, into another language. Alexandria as the very type of cosmopolis, the city of learning that will always be threatened by barbarians, and always succumbs — that barbarians may acquire virtue by invasion — is a symbol of what is done by version and translation.

Translation and version entail meditation on between-ness, each a turning or carrying across from one thing to another; given the fluid instability of utterance, the lack of an original grounding, it is an exact intent that has "Versions" lead the reader "Between the Symplegades", those wandering rocks that belie, as vanity and illusion, the very notions of substance, solidity and stasis. Where there is reflection, there is much water, which is now the water of voyaging: Casey's use of water in its aspects of voyaging and reflection alludes with shimmering suggestiveness to Whitman's "Crossing Brooklyn Ferry" — as that poem alludes to the Greek from which Casey translates. In this instance the Greek poem, Seferis' *Mythological Story*, is a densely-wrought and intensely self-reflective re-vision of Greek themes, corded loosely by the voyage of the Argonauts. As in Cavafy's "Ithaka" the voyage of Ulysses is a quest for self and self-knowledge, so in the sequence of Seferis there is no explicit Golden Fleece: all the objects of quests are symbols of self-uncovering, that which reveals the innermost as transcendent: a transcendence, echoing as presence in these poems in the reiterated sounding of the word "beyond". No poem can successfully move from the Fleece or Ithaka, (or the Grail) to the trandescence which is thereby symbolized — for the symbol holds in common what in transcendence are disparate destinies. Avoiding transcendent meanings, the great poems end by attending to the actuality of Ithaka or the loaded encrustations of the Golden Fleece. "Between the Symplegades" is almost pure sequence where the individual ending knows no resolution but, beyond peace, the continuity of flux. "Resolution" is too strong a word to translate *Dikaiosyne*, "an attunement of opposite tensions", or a balance in which two weights are not even, and therefore cancelled out, but wherein each is allowed the full force of its gravitational pull.

If we think of "symbol" in its etymological sense, as of a putting together, or that which is formed when two are thrown together (like a indenture), we can see how Seferis and Casey, make use of the Symplegades whose root meaning is "clashers together". The necessary way is to sail between those which clash together — or we might say, to sustain *dikaiosyne* of the between and the together, of the one always threatened by two and the two always about to become one. There is a further complexity of symmetry (if that is not too exact a word) between the Wandering Rocks — as the Symplegades are often called — and the wandering of the voyagers:

we thought we knew

there were beautiful islands

somewhere round here

close by

perhaps here

or a little further on

no — just here

where we are groping

> (VIII *old ships*)

As this voyaging, so compounded of the inner and the outer, instructs us, the urge to seek is born out of the failure to bring to realization "here". The mystery is within, and between.

Between languages, between cultures, and between faiths: Gerard Casey has been an explorer of the archaic roots of Christianity, and an apprehender of the truth to which different religions approximate, and for which they strive. That we know so much as to be condemned to what others call "relativism" is in part a consequence of our belatedness: we survey the manifestations and the history of religion and the imagination from the privileged heights of detachment: we are free to choose, yet choice invites scepticism. Hinduism, Buddhism, the Tao, the spiritual intimations of classical mythology, and the esoteric faith of mystics all have a place in Casey's poetry. Not being systematic, such a gathering is open to the charge of eclectism — a charge that I trust any reading of the poetry to refute. We find a quality more responsible and more profound — the acknowledgement of the uncertainties in the most compelling faith and of the Spirit's transgressive listful borderlessness.

> late news
>
> South Wales Echo
>
> late night news . . .

Our news is late, and all we get is an echo from an earlier age: yet the echo is enough, all that has ever been heard. The pun on the name of the Cardiff newspaper is wonderfully suggestive, but more even than that it is a pun about punning, for punning is a form of echo, as we find in Herbert's "Heaven":

> O, who will show me those delights on high?
>
> Echo: *I.*
>
> Thou Echo, thou art mortal, all men know.
>
> Echo: *No.*

By a pun the banality and commonplaceness of the paperboy's call is simultaneously a call of transcendence, an echo of the divine — and we are reminded again of the acoustic materiality of voice. As sacrament is *not* a transformation of one thing into another but the simultaneity of both bread and wine, H_2O and the water of life, so voice is *not* the transformation of chords and vibrations into meaning but the joint presence of both words and the means of their conveyance and representation.

Belatedness is further endorsed by the poem's epigraph from one of Donne's *Holy Sonnets,* "What if this present were the world's last night?" This will certainly be a poem of revelation, for apocalypse is the end-time when all the echoes meet. If this is an echo of eternity, of the divine, heard in South Wales, then, like every echo, it partakes and carries within it that divine eternity. It is thus an echo *of* apocalypse which is also, necessarily, an echo heard *at* apocalypse, an echo returning to its original Word.

Such ambiguity is a feature of typology, that form of narrative and interpretation that brings together earlier and later, that has the latter foreshadowed in the former, and the former fulfilled in the latter. We hear the Fall in:

> down Adam's Down
>
> down Adam's
>
> down . . .

and see the shadow of Golgotha in the hanging of the accused men. Shadows, like echoes, contain within and partake of that which precedes (falls in front of) them. Through the Incarnation it becomes axiomatic of Christian typology that it not be retrospective: the three condemned men do not look back to Golgotha, but require us to see Golgotha brought up to the present, made present here, that Christ may be present in "the least of these my brethren". That we are left uncertain of the guilt or innocence of Jim (Mary Anne's husband; Jesus was the son and grandson of Mary and Anne) puts us in the position of the mob, challenged by Pilate to judge, and to judge for ourselves — and in doing that — judging ourselves. As echo is contained in Aristophanes' chorus of frogs, "brekek*ekex koa*x", so it is heard also in the equally absurd proclamation of Pilate: "Ecce Homo!" Metathesis gives us echoes of home (the poet's childhood home) from "Ecce Homo!", just as by spiritual analogue to metathesis the Incarnation enables Paul to speak of "Not I, but Christ in me". As the devices of rhetoric, such as puns, echoes and metathesis (all much used by Biblical writers and early Church Fathers, and integral to the Christian notion of fallen language: see Michael Edwards, *Towards a Christian Poetics*, 1984) destabilize and give fluidity to language, so the Incarnation destroys the barriers of individual identity, so that those baptised into Christ have put on Christ, that Christ may be all in all. Destabilized language, full of tricks and traps, is a consequence of the Fall, and of Babel, but it is also a way of redemption. The folly is to suppose that language is, ought, or could be pure mediation, whose fixity as "ordinary language" can be the ground of philosophy: this is deliciously mocked by Casey in two lines:

<blockquote>

babble on Bert babble on

babble on in air

</blockquote>

in which we hear Babel, Babylon, Bertrand Russell and leaves rustling in the wind of Ayer. "Ordinary language" philosophy can argue logically with symbols, but it is impotent in the presence of puns, of language misbehaving.

Languages's most scandalous transgression, the Word becoming flesh, is the antithesis and reversal of man's transgression and fall. When the Word becomes flesh the fleshliness, materiality and acoustical and visual properties of words become redeemable. Readers are not likely to understand the Welsh (to which however translations are provided in the notes), but we can figure out the Greek and guess at the Hebrew. That would be our educated instinct. Instead we should do what a foreign tongue enables us to do easily, and attend to the look and sound of words apart from their meaning, their supposed semantic equivalence in translation. Eliot, Pound, David Jones, Hugh MacDiarmid — to take Casey's most immediate antecedents — do not challenge our linguistic competence but rather our ability to see and hear words as they are, not as they mean. This is a poem to be looked at — the disposition of types and scripts is always to be reckoned — and, equally, a poem to be heard in all its tongues and voices. And when, reading aloud, we come to the Hebrew our silence utters the ineffable. Few readers will be trained to read the Hebrew "backwards", from right to left, and yet out of that cultural assumption of normative scriptorial behaviour Casey makes drama. Right to left here is at once a reversal of direction in movement and a crossing of left to right, as the cry of the seraphim is silenced on the Cross until the Resurrection which is also revocation — the unsilencing of echo, the unforgetting (anathemata) of prophesy. In these cross-wise scripts we have an alphabetic analogy of chiasmus, the rhetorical figure of crossing and reversal, of echoic doubling and inverting, that Christian writers (from the New Testament on) have recognized as their own intimate trope. For all that, many readers will be unable to pronounce, rather than to decode, the Hebrew words which are, to those outside, not words but hieroglyphs. And insofar as a hieroglyph, a secret, durable scratching, resists our pronunciation, so far does it incarnate the stubbornness of stone, the near absolute degree of silence. In the seraphic proclamation, language and silence cross.

The recalcitrance of stone is, according to Ezekiel, Isaiah and the mystic Ruysbroek (see note 5), also the radiance of Christ: the absolute density of matter is a measure of the absolution of the Incarnation. The Christianity of "South Wales Echo" is cosmic and all-redeeming, enfolding and encompassing all, allowing nothing to be cast into outer darkness. The night that descends at the poem's end, in the luminous gloss of the opening of John's gospel, cannot "comprehend" the light, leaves always the "Nightlight Glow" that from Adam's Down can only lead up. Instead of the dualistic or Gnostic struggle between light and dark, the Christian myth, as expounded by John, insists on the absoluteness of light. It is odd, therefore, that the doctrine of cosmic reparation or final restitution, "apokatastasis", has been associated with Origen and condemned as a heresy of gnostic derivation. As is made explicit in some of Gerard Casey's essays (of which two are included in this volume) apokatastasis is central to the poet's apprehension of Christianity. If there were any person so evil as to be unredeemable, even Satan himself, then the darkness would have overcome the light. That this doctrine is central to early Christian thought is shown by the inclusion in the Creed, with minimal support from scripture, of Christ's descent into Hell, that in the Resurrection he might restore the entirety of creation.

Although condemned as a heresy in the writings of Origen, the doctrine of apokatastasis is to be found in many other early Christian writers, most obviously in St. Gregory of Nyssa. The problem is that there is an apparent contradiction between this doctrine and some of the "hard parables" of Jesus, about, for example, the division between sheep and goats and the Last Judgment. Wrongly stressing such passages from the Gospels, and neglecting the consonance with apokatastasis in the opening of John's gospel, in Paul's letter to the Ephesians ("anakephalaiosis", 1:10), in creeds and post-apostolic writings, St. Jerome was able, disastrously, to introduce as Christian doctrine such cheap worldliness, such petty concern from the mundane order as this: "If there is to be such a restitution of all things (apokatastasis), will there be, then, no distinction between virgin and harlot?"

At the very heart of the doctrine of apokatastasis is the more familiar doctrine of the Fall and the Redemption, by which each sinner, i.e. every man, will be redeemed. Jerome and Augustine introduced (from civil law, presumably) the normality of innocence, the supposition that a virgin is — metaphysically, ontologically, in the eyes of God less fallen than a harlot. If we are to understand Christianity as a universal and cosmic religion then these expoundings of Augustine and Jerome must be treated as a local aberration but alas with consequences far from local. Poets, notably Blake and Milton — have understood the irreducible value of experience, the superiority of redemption over primary innocence. It is not only wise to believe this but also pragmatic, for there can be no return to the state of Eden. What Adam did not possess in Eden was discernment, and that is something to be learned from the fall into experience, as we find in Blake, and in Vaughan, a poet always aware of the cosmos, the universal and of the limitlessness of redemption. It is in the darkness of Vaughan's "Night", and only there, that the true light can be distinguished from the false:

> Wise Nicodemus saw such light
> As made him know his God by night.

In the darkness of fall we find the nightlight glow, so that in Vaughan's poem the darkness is barely separable from God:

> There is in God (some say)
> A deep, but dazzling darkness . . .

Is not that haunting parenthesis a rumour, an echo of apokatastasis?

"South Wales Echo" enacts the dazzle of its own dark obscurities. By no means an easy poem, it is an inexhaustible one. As we re-read it, new echoes will come to ear, shadow will disclose form. In the very parity of obscure luminosities "South Wales Echo" responds to the work of David Jones, to whom it is so exactly dedicated. In David Jones, more than in any other recent poet, we reckon difficulty as the price of comprehensiveness, incomprehension as the only fit expression of that which comprehends all, even the dark. The darkness of our own reading, the inadequacy of our understanding — in "South Wales Echo" as in *The Anathemata* — humbles us to the fall, and uncovers the lasting residue of darkness — points of light, τό φῶς, lights that point "beyond": yonder we follow now we follow. Yonder . . .

Charles Lock
Toronto

Versions

for Anna Dimascio

ἀλλ' ἐκδιδάσκει πάνθ' ὁ γηράσκων χρόνος.

Aeschylus, Prometheus Bound 982

voices

in our hearts
in dreams
voices call
again and again
faintly echoing
from long-forgotten mornings

in dreams
voices echo
faraway nightmusic
from another shore
from death's other shore
lost voices
loved voices . . .

(after Cavafy)

nightmusic

Alexandria
outside Cleopatra's palace
night
watchmen's voices:

List, list!

Hark!

Music i' the air

under the earth . . .

It signs well does it not?

No.

Peace, I say!

What should this mean. . . ?

How now?

How now! Do you hear this?

Ay; is't not strange?

Content. 'Tis strange . . .

(after Shakespeare 'Anthony and Cleopatra' 4:3/Plutarch 'Anthony' LXXV:3.4)

the god abandons Anthony

when suddenly at midnight you hear voices
and music: boding exquisite
and unseen revellers pass
do not lament: your luck given out at last
all that you have striven to do, to be and failed
all your plans, once so alluring, that have played you false
do not fruitlessly grieve
like a brave man, like a man long ready
say goodbye to the Alexandria you are losing

O do not say: I was mistaken, I heard nothing, it was a dream
do not deceive yourself
rather remember
you were thought worthy of such a city
you are no coward . . . no prayers, no complaints
like one long prepared
go to the window and stand quietly, listen
it is your last delight
and, as the unseen revellers pass,
listen to that nightmusic
secret, inviolable, boding
and say goodbye to Alexandria
she is leaving

(after Cavafy)

the city

you say:

'I will go to another land, another sea
another city better than this
I have tried, I have failed
I am condemned, written off
my heart is a lump, dead and buried
must I stay in this . . . death?
I look about me, see
black ruin . . . wasted years'

listen:

'for you there are no new places, new seas
the city is within you, you take it with you
you are the city
in its houses, streets
among such neighbours
you will always be, grow old, grey
this is your city
you cannot escape
for you there is no road out
no ship to another land
go as you will
you will always reach again
this city'

(after Cavafy)

Megistias

all honour to Megistias the seer at Thermopylae
and all those who stand
at the burning gates
in defence of freedom
unmoved in the face of death

equal to themselves
just and generous-hearted at all times
straightforward and compassionate
lending a hand insofar as they are able
truthful yet untouched by hatred of those who lie

all honour too — yes even greater honour —
to those who can only stand and wait
they also serve yet know
truth will be betrayed
the barbarian will break through at last . . .

(after Simonides/Cavafy)

Ithaka

now when over the ocean
that brightest of stars rose
which ever comes
to herald the light of early dawn
even then the seafaring ship
drew near to the island
and Odysseus woke out of his sleep
and springing up stood
and looking out on his native land
groaned and cried out:

'Woe, woe . . . to what land am I now come . . . ?'

(after Homer: Odyssey)

Ithaka

when you set sail on the voyage to Ithaka
pray that the way be long
full of adventures, full of surprises
surly Poseidon? don't be afraid of him!
mock his anger
the Laestrygonians, the Cyclops
Polyphemus — these you carry within you
your own heart sets them before you
do not fear them

pray that your journey be long
that many a glorious morning
with joy, with delight
you sail into unknown harbours
drop anchor at Phoenician ports
and search out beautiful merchandise
mother-of-pearl and coral
amber and ebony and ivory
and delicate perfumes
yes delicate perfumes and every kind of lovely fabric
pray that you will come to know many cities
many Egyptian cities, learn many things
gather stores of wisdom from the wise

Ithaka will always be in your mind
don't doubt you will arrive there
but do not hurry your journey in the least
pray rather it will last you many years and bring you wealth
and grown old at last drop anchor
in the harbour at Ithaka

arrived there you will find Ithaka
has nothing to offer any longer
but she is no cheat
she has not deceived you
to her you owe your voyage
all your wealth, all your wisdom
and you will know
the meaning of Ithaka

(after Cavafy)

Damis of Nysa

Antipater at Sidon
to his friend Meleager at Cos:

our friend
Damis of Nysa
in a snowstorm
running his small boat
through icy winds and waves
across the Ionian sea
to the land of Pelops
brought his ship cargo and friends
safe to safe harbour . . .
even as the anchor was cast
the old man slumping over
chilled to the bone
sank into the haven of Lethe

(after Antipater of Sidon)

Nigel Harbour

Nigel Harbour, Norwegian, pilot at Colombo
gave safe passage out of harbour
to ships leaving for unknown ports
far away on the other side of the world
would climb down, silent and thoughtful, into his boat
cross to the crossbench
smoking an old clay pipe
muttering to himself
arms crossed on his chest
muttering in a northern tongue
as the ships were lost to sight

Nigel Harbour, old captain of cargo boats
voyaging, crossed the round world
one day felt tired
stayed on in Colombo as pilot to the harbour
he was always thinking of far-off islands
the Lofoten Islands
legended islands in the northern ocean

one day in his pilot-boat
returning to harbour —
clear passage given to the tanker Fjord Folden
bound for the Lofoten Islands —
as she sank
smoke-down over the horizon
he pulled out his pipe
muttered under his breath
slipped to the side
and was suddenly still

(after N. Kabbadias)

anamnesis

as far as this I have come
this mark
O call it what you will
scar birthmark deathmark target omen sign
this spot this place
where youth wrestles with the wind
face to face
on the rocks by the sea

where is a man to go
who is only a man
counting his moments visions voices heard
reckoning his wings against remorse
a child turning into a man
always near the sea
the seagull a flickering shadow
under the sun he learns to breathe

yes I have come as far as this
adding up: white to a black total
a tree here and there
one or two wet pebbles
light fingers a gentle touch on the forehead
what forehead?

all night they wept — my hopes
and are gone — not one left
I listen for — a free footstep
an untired voice in the morning
splashing at the jetty
under the sterns of boats
bearing names in darker blue
against the horizon
a few years a few waves
quiet rowing in the harbours

I have come to this
a groove in the sand
to be washed away
two eyes in the silence
touch me bring me light
blot out a thousand worlds
I remember other suns
suns nearer the light
remember in my blood
nearer the light
a smile atones for flame

but here — a sinking coast
edging a pitiless sea
in this dead land hope withers
a sudden flurry of feathers dizzy
in the dust caked under impatient feet
ash from old volcanic fires
Hephaestus dead

here I am
hardened to stone
an offering to the sea
a pierced pebble vowed to the waters
beyond the islands
under the waves
brother to anchor stones

where the keels cut the waves
assert their mastery
where the porpoise plunges
and leaps to the rising sun
the nets draw in a doll
painfully wrought
salt indifferent white
its blank gaze turned
to the immeasurable sea

(after Odysseus Elytis)

a song for Dionysus

in these gleaming courtyards
where the wind whistles through the arches
that tree — shaking rustling quivering wilfully laughing
red blossoms shivering in triumph leaping in the dawnlight
tell me tell me — is that the mad pomegranate tree?

on these plains where naked girls with light yellow arms
are wandering in dreams harvesting clover
what puts the lights in their bright green baskets
filling them to the brim with singing birds
what showers glory against the clouds above them?
tell me tell me — is that the mad pomegranate tree?

adorning itself jealously with seven sorts of feathers
reflecting the sun with a thousand blinding prisms
seizing at the gallop the horse's mane savagely lashing
laughing singing crying out new hope dawning
tell me — is that the mad pomegranate tree?

that tree waving in the distance
a thousand leaves cool green flowers at the sea's edge
that sea where waves flow to unknown shores
teeming to birth with numberless ships
is that the mad pomegranate tree?

that creaks the rigging high in the shining air
that breaks on the masts bunches of blue grapes
flaring arrogant dangerous celebrating
shattering with light the black storm at the world's centre

spreading the golden ruffle of day scattering song
that which ravishes entices allures obsesses
rages against evil black darkness
spilling birdsong in sunlight branching out
opening its wings in deepest dreams
is that the mad pomegranate tree?

(after Odysseus Elytis)

at the church door

that Saturday night —
at the first shiver of light
over Adonis dead —
all the candles were lit
a wave of light
ran from the Sanctuary to the door
and all were chanting:
'Christ is risen'

suddenly, in shaking hands
the candles flickered
the hair rose on their heads
all faces turned to the door
and a voice screamed:
'Oh Mrs George look! There's Vangelis'

and there stood Vangelis
the young blood, the young gallant
darling of all the girls in the village —
he'd been lost in the war —
there he was with a wooden leg
stiff on his crutches
standing at the church door . . .

Vangelis the dancer —
how he'd shaken the threshing floors
at the harvest dances —
there he stood still as a statue
they all stared at Vangelis
in the darkening light —
the candles going out one by one
in the draught from the door —
stared at Vangelis
stared at his face
stared at his leg
nailed to the spot
not coming in

(after Angelos Sikelianos)

an open question

h'm
what's this?
nothing inside
just   empty . . .

limestone
looks shaped
nothing outside
just   nothing . . .

cenotaph?
anchorhold?
cross-in-hand?

Stylite's pillar?
sarcophagus?
Lot's wife?

or — with a friendly glance
at the ghost of Charlie
modern times?

think

no don't think — no need for that —
take a shot in the dark

guess

any answers?

(after Agathias Scholasticus)

monotone

'. . . the same yesterday and today and forever . . .'

(Hebrews 13:8)

Koheleth to Heraclitus:

the same   the same   the same
      days creep on from days

days   and days   and days
      come in from yesterdays

tomorrow   and tomorrow   and tomorrow
      so day creeps on from day

tomorrow brings in months brings in years
in months in years are all our yesterdays

now?

now is all
all that is past or passing or to come

now?

now is nothing
no thing new under the sun

no need to guess
no need to look

nothing . . .

'Paul opened his eyes and saw nothing . . .'

(Eckhart)

(after Cavafy/see: Heraclitus, Bywater VII)

north wind

thin snow falling
a chill wind blowing
stiff lambs freezing
outside on the hills

on a cot
through flying clouds
through gaps in the roof
fierce and glittering
stars stare down

a child moaning
fretfully tossing
the mother weeping

'O Father O Mother
leave my child
it is only one
the others you have taken'

what terrible message
was the north wind bringing?

(after George Zalokostas)

the old violin

the old violin is playing
in the winter night
playing playing
in the cold winter night

as the night grows colder colder
who is playing on the old violin
playing playing
as the night grows colder
darker . . . ?

(after John Polemis)

sleep

take me away
still the pain
at my heart

let rest come
deep and dreamless
forgetful of all ill

with small butterfly touch
close my eyes
take me away
sleep . . .

(after John Gryparis)

death

come
with no wild storm
close my eyes quietly

let it be spring
apple blossom falling
in gardens and orchards

let it be sunset
a gentle wind blowing
to my heart
let the loved voices call
the old voices

(after John Gryparis)

the other shore

O to reach the green shore
the other shore
there we shall sleep sweetly

the old sky the old stars
will drift away
a smile touch our lips
as gently the wind
from the other shore
blows to the heart

yes we shall sleep
like children exhausted
fallen asleep after long weeping

the girls of our village
the wild pear trees
whispering will tell
of happy years

the oldest friend
the long-loved one
will greet us

all bitterness
will fall away
as in a story
told long ago . . .

(after Constantine Karyotakis)

Easter Morning

the day is cool
the last star heralding
a day of purest sunshine
no mist, no cloud moving
across the sky
a wind blowing
gently breathing to the heart speaks:
death is dark but life is honey-sweet!

O! be ready
everyone of you
old and young
men and women
little and big
maidens and children
everyone of you
gather in joy
in the bay-covered churches
lift your arms
before the icons
gather in peace
embrace — and — all of you —
cry out
'Christ is risen!'

see
bayleaves on all the tombs
happy babies in their mothers' arms
old faces in candlelight
the choristers chanting
gleaming of gold
flashing of silver
every face shining
in the light
shed from the candles
we hold in our hands
before the icons
and the choristers chanting
'Christ is risen!'

listen!
all of you   Christ is risen!
everyone of you   Christ is risen!
listen!   Christ is risen!

(after Dionysios Solomos)

43

the old violin

listen to the old violin
in the April night
playing playing
in the quiet April night

as it grows older
worms gnaw the wood
yet sweeter stronger
sounds the voice
of the lonely violin
in the still April night

as the year grows colder
listen to the old violin
in the silent autumn night
its voice grows stranger
wilder wilder
singing of love
as it grows older

(after John Polemis)

nightfall

beyond the window
the black cypress tree
at the end of the garden
held in the empty sky

nothing more

(after Kostis Palamas/Mary Casey)

Between the Symplegades

Re-Visions from
A MYTHOLOGICAL STORY
by George Seferis

for Jeremy Hooker

ἔστιν θάλασσα, τίς δέ νιν κατασβέσει;

Aeschylus, Agamemnon 958

Note

'*A Mythological Story*' *is a sequence of twenty-four poems by George Seferis published at Athens in 1935 under the title* Mythistorema. *The text may be found in the* Collected Poems 1924–1955 *introduced, edited and translated by Edmund Keeley and Philip Sherrard (Jonathan Cape 1969). This edition has a foreword which serves as a valuable introduction to the poetry of Seferis and some helpful notes on the text. The translations are literal and straightforward and an adequate support for readers not fluent in the original language.*

Kimon Friar, the distinguished translator of modern Greek poetry into English, has defined translation as 'a form of relationship between two poems in different languages when one of the two can only flourish after the other has preceded it and prepared the way for it'. If this definition — which Kimon Friar claims is the best definition of the translation of poetry he knows — is accepted, the versions printed here may be called translations. As however the aim has been to present a free interpretation of the poems as they struck one particular reader the description 'Re-Visions' has been preferred.

In the interests of this interpretation two poems from elsewhere in the work of Seferis have been introduced into the sequence. These are 'Erotikos Logos B', which appears under the title 'The Appled Tree', introducing the Acheron sequence, and 'Euripides the Athenian' from Logbook III which appears juxtaposed to 'Mythistorema k' (Andromeda). Also 'Orestes' has been placed to follow 'Astyanax' instead of immediately preceding it as in the original sequence.

'The mythology of the ancient world plays a crucial role in Seferis.' (Keeley and Sherrard: Foreword p.ix). Readers unfamiliar with this mythology may turn for help to the Keeley and Sherrard edition together with a classical dictionary. A comment from Seferis himself may be repeated here:

> *'men of inconstancy, of wanderings and wars, though they differ and may change in terms of greatness and value . . . always move among the same monsters and the same longings. So we keep the symbols and the names that the myth has brought down to us realising as we do that the typical characters have changed in keeping with the passing of time and the different conditions of our world — which are none other than the conditions of everyone who seeks expression.'*

> *(quoted by Keeley and Sherrard: Foreword p.ix)*

Two further comments seem necessary.

Hydra *(Eumenides III): apart from its mythological associations, which are relevant here, Hydra as the immediate subject of the poem is a rocky island off the coast of the Peloponnese. It played a vital part in the naval struggle during the Greek War of Independence in the early nineteenth century. Colourful annual celebrations commemorating the struggle take place there.*

Δικαιοσύνη: *this word, with which 'Argonauts' closes has been left untranslated as any possible equivalents carry unacceptable connotations in English. Here the word is used in an Heraclitean sense indicating the balance of all opposing tensions as resolved in the Whole: 'an attunement of opposite tensions as of the bow or lyre ; the name of the bow is life, its work is death . . . ' (Heraclitus: Fragments LVI and LXVI. Bywater)*

THE SYMPLEGADES

I

the messenger

the messenger —
three years we waited, watching
the pines, the beach, the stars
one with the ploughshare, the ship's keel
we hoped to find seed again
that the ancient story might be told once more

we came back — broken
legs, arms no longer capable
mouths soured by rust, by brine
strangers to ourselves
bruised by swans — those spotless wings —
and waking
plunged into mists
journeyed to the north

in winter
through long nights
maddened by winds
intolerably blowing from the east

in summer
through long days lost
an agony that could not die

we brought back
these writings
carved out, engraved on tablets
a humble craft

II

grooves

once more — a well
deep in a cave
I remember
long ago it was easy to draw up something
an image perhaps
or some piece of finery that pleased our friends
those who remembered us

but the rope is broken
only the grooves on the well's rim
bring to mind past happiness
the finger on the lip
(so the poet puts it)

under feverish fingers
the stone is cool to the touch

the cave ventures its soul
loses it

the moments pass

silence

not a drop of water

III

the muttering head

I wake up: in my hands this Medusan head
it tires me, exhausts me: it gives me no rest
I cannot put it down
as I was waking it fell into my dream
it is now one with me — inseparable
I look at the eyes: not open, not closed
I speak to it: the mouth tries to answer, mutters
I clutch at the cheeks: they bulge behind the skin

I have no strength left

for a moment
my hands are lost

they are with me again

mutilated

IV

Argonauts

in the mirror we see
the enemy and the stranger
soul to know itself looks into soul

the crew, our companions, were good lads
unchanging in the changing days
they did not grumble at the labour
the thirsts, the night frosts
like trees, like waves
they accepted the wind, the rain
the night-cold, the heat of the sun
through long days with downcast eyes
breathing in unison
blood tingling the clear skin
they sweated at the oar

once with lowered eyes they sang at sunset
as we swiftly passed the empty island
beyond the cape of dogs that howl
the island where barbary figs grow
they would say — to know itself
let soul look into soul
and their oars would strike the golden sea
as the sun was setting
among gulls and seals
we went beyond many capes, many islands
passed over the sea that flows into the other sea
there were times when unhappy women
cried out from the shores
lamenting children lost
and other voices calling wildly over the sea
babbled of Alexander the Great
and glories hidden in the depths of Asia

we would anchor in bays
among the singing of birds
by waters that left on the hands
memories of a great happiness
and air full of night-scents

but there was never an end of journeying
voyaging their souls became one
with the oars and rowlocks
with the grave figure at the prow
with the wake of the rudder
with the water endlessly fracturing
their image

one by one they died
their eyes still lowered
oars mark the places
they lie on the beaches

no one remembers them

Δικαιοσύνη

V

beyond stone images

no — we did not know them
it must have been hope that whispered
'we have known them since we were children'

they went off in ships
with cargoes of coal, of grain
we saw them perhaps twice . . . then
they were lost beyond the ocean
we never saw them again

now, by tired light in the mornings
on sheets of paper we try to draw
clumsily, wearily
ships, mermaids, shells

in the evening dusk
we go down to the river
it flows to the sea
we pass the nights in cellars
breathing in the smell of tar

they have left us
did we ever see them?
perhaps only in a dream
when sleep brought us to the edge
of the heaving wave

perhaps in seeking them
we seek another life

beyond stone images

VI

behind clouded glass

from the low window
from behind clouded glass
you will see the garden
see the fountains in the rain

the garden with its fountains
will be for you
a glimpse of the other life
beyond tragic columns
beyond broken images

the misty glass
will cut you off
from the chorus
among the bitter laurels
growing along the edges
of new quarries

earth and sap of trees
springing in memory will strike
the window struck by the rain
from the outer world
as you cease to breathe

in the firelit room
far away lightnings will light up
your wrinkled head

VII

south wind

waiting
maddened by the wind
intolerably blowing from the south
shredding the flesh on our bones
from these windows among the pines and carobs
we stare out at the mountains in the west
floating beyond the sea

writing on tables beside us
many letters — so many letters over so many months
writing to you
trying to reach across — to fill the gap
dropping our letters into the void
writing each of us the same things

we fall silent in each others' presence
each of us alone and separate
watching the light and dark
moving along the mountains
and you

when you shine down on us
our hours are sweeter than oil
on healing wounds
than cold water to the thirsting palate
than the peace descending
under the slow wings of journeying swans

you hold us
in the palms of your hands
in the nights
in the bitterness of exile
as we crouch under the white wall
your voice comes to us
fire to our hopes
but again this wind cuts
razor-keen against our nerves

O this constriction at the heart
who will lift it from us?
yesterday a downpour of rain in the evening

and now again a heavy sky, a weight above us
our thoughts — threshing down uselessly
like yesterday's pinedrenched rainstorm
in front of our doorway —
seek to prop up a falling tower

on this bare headland open to the south
to the wind
as we stare out at the mountains in front of us
hiding you
who among the decimated villages
will count the cost for us
of our decision to forget?

who will accept our offering?

autumn moves on to winter

VIII

old ships

here — on the crowded decks of old ships
ships barely holding together
among sallow women and fractious children
unable to forget ourselves for a moment
unseeing of swallow-fish
or stars at the mast-heads

gramophones brokenly crooning, grating
caught up in unreal pilgrimages
what are we looking for . . . always voyaging?

always moving on sea-rotted planks
from harbour to harbour

moving broken stones
crumbling at the jetties
each passing day breathing less easily
the pine trees' fragrance
swimming in this sea, in that sea
at the edge of a land
no longer ours
or yours

no communion

alone

we thought we knew
there were beautiful islands
somewhere round here
close by

perhaps here
or a little farther on

no — just here
where we are groping

IX

beyond the asphodels

waiting in this old harbour
I think of those who went off
one to the island of plane trees
one to the island of pine trees
and that other who left for the open sea

there can be no more waiting

trying to make up my mind
to come back to life —
with the smell of the salt
from that other storm
still in the sail-cloths
rust from the old cannon
still on my hands
I touch fearfully the oars

I wanted to be alone: a solitude
I did not expect this foreboding
this breaking of soul against . . .
the sea-colour, the silence
the horizon line

Odysseus waiting for the dead
I think of him at night under the stars
think too of Adonis in that gorge, dead
anchored here as I am
beyond the asphodels

X

between the Symplegades

our country is shut in
we live
day and night
under a low sky
pent among mountains
no rivers, no wells, no springs

we have one or two cisterns
empty and echoing
echoes, muffled stagnant dull
heavy
as our loneliness our love our bodies —
we worship them

once we could build
houses huts sheepfolds
that is strange
our marriages — the wreaths and rings
our children born, grown strong
these are enigmas
they baffle our souls

on Sunday
we go down to the harbour to breathe
see, lit in the sunset,
broken planks
bodies that no longer remember —
love forgotten —
débris from voyages that never ended

our country is shut in — caught
between the two black Symplegades

THE EUMENIDES

I

white wings

you grew cold
like the moon in the endless night
your blood froze, spread
white wings over
black rocks, the shapes of trees and houses

long ago we knew
we were children once
a little light

II

bottle in the sea

embittered —
the deep places are unsearchable
infolded on boundless calm —
at the edge of the trackless sea
we tie up the ship
patch broken oars
drink water, sleep
under three rocks, a few burnt pines
a solitary place of prayer

above all is repeated
again three rocks
corroded rusted
a track between pines
seared, black and livid

and beyond
a square hut
buried in whitewash

and is again repeated
again and again
level on level
to the horizon
to the evening sky

here we threw dice
for a coin found among the pebbles
the youngest won it
and was lost to us

we set out again
with broken oars

throw this bottle into the sea

III

Hydra

look! the sea
once so bitter to you
blue, dark with white wings
full of colours in the sun

heaving swaying rolling
tossing the glittering many-coloured ships

dolphins flags cannons booming
sails white in the sunlight
oars dripping on stilled waves
striking to the rhythm of drums

O if only you would look
your eyes would grow beautiful again
your arms stretch out bright and glowing
your lips live again
looking at such a wonder

why don't you look?

what were you looking for in the ashes
in the rain in the fog in the wind
in the ruins
when the lights were going out
when the city was falling
when from the stone pavements
one showed you his heart

what were you looking for

what . . . ?

IV

pigeons

ends written in the light
colours and gestures
people we have loved

three blood-red pigeons
tumbling in the light

V

beyond sleep

sleep holds you
enfolded in green leaves
you breathe like a tree
in the quiet light

I see your image
in the clear spring
eyes closed
lashes writ in water

in the grass
my fingers find your fingers
feel your pulse
know for a moment
in another place
your heart's pain

under the plane trees
among the laurels
at the water's edge
sleep moves you
brings you nearer me
wrapped in silence

I cannot touch you

your shadow grows
then dwindles
lost among the shadows
in that other world that leaves you free
yet holds you

the life given us we have lived

pity those who so patiently wait
lost under the plane trees
among the black laurels
those who speak to springing wells
drown among the circling voices
as the springing wells talk louder

pity the one without hope
who shared our privations
our hurt: then like a crow
plunged black into the sun

grant us
beyond the ruins
beyond sleep

peace

VI

Astyanax

you are leaving
take the boy with you
that day when the trumpets sounded
and weapons flashed —
the horses were at the troughs
nostrils dripping over the green water —
he saw the light under the plane tree

the knotted olive trees, the rocks
that knew our fathers
our brothers alive on the earth
were a rich pattern, a living joy —
for those of us who knew how to pray

you are leaving
no one knows whom he will kill
how he will die

this breaking day
will cancel all debts

take the boy with you —
he will remember
the light under the leaves
of that plane tree

VII

Orestes

in black rows, in crowds they watch me
roar at my uplifted hand
raised triumphant above the chariot
as I circle the bloodstained track

watch me still
as again and again
I circle the track

the axle creaks, burns
smokes into flame

flecked with foam
the reins stretched to breaking
I reach out over the maddened horses
will they never weary
will ever again their hooves
fall flush to the ground
on the soft grass
among the poppies
where in spring you picked a daisy?

your eyes were shining
we did not know where to look
(I have no country)

my knees weaken, buckle
over the axle the wheels the wild track
when the gods will
knees buckle
strength doesn't count

none can escape the cradle
this trial by hatred

remember the flute-song in autumn

without forgiveness
you cannot find the sea
for all your galloping horses
for all your circling
past the black rows
the bored ones
the Eumenides

ACHERON

I

the appled tree

the secrets of the sea are forgotten
at the sea's edge
foam rides light on the deep places
flecked on the darkness
on the black reefs . . . but memory
the unforgetting
rises at a sudden gleam

O to bring back that dawn
the light that was living
then flowers might spring again
days ripen under an open heaven
those eyes shine in the answering light
soul pure as flute-song

hands touching we made a bridge
for two destinies
levelled in the untired light
to cross
the wind knew but snatched at us
the unknowing

O be still . . . remember
how slight — barely realized — the movement
the beginning
your hand reached out, touching
offending hurting
the appled tree
dread, spinning the thread
pointing the way, led you on
O dark shudder at the roots
the leaves shivering

the twang of a bow
a stifled cry . . . and
night fell on closing eyes
ashes and dizziness
encircling
the darkening glass

a flutter of wings
no man can guess at

the wind blows hot
the shade is narrow
under the cypress trees
all round the mountains rise steeply

they weary us
those who do not know
how to die

our friends

II

autumn wind

I sink in stone
all I loved
vanished with the bright summer houses
blown away by the wind
last autumn

grieving
I let the river flow through my fingers
lifted not a drop
to my lips

beside me
in the red soil
a tiny seedling grows

III

Andromeda

the sea the sea
who shall drain it dry?

the sinking rocks
drag me with them

day breaks
hands beckon
to the vulture
to the hawk

again
the wound opens
at the heart

black and still
the dead trees breathe

the stone images smile
frozen

the stars set
in my veins

the footsteps of men
fall in silence
grow fainter

silence

Euripides

between
the fires of Troy
the quarries of Syracuse
caught
he lived grew old

he haunted caves
at the sea's edge

a net
a snare for beasts
he'd try to break

so he saw
the veins of men

a crabbed man
cross-grained
his friends were few

in time rent
savaged by dogs
he died

Euripides

Athenian

IV

the dead

forgetting ourselves for a moment
we looked at the broken images
and said:

life is not so easily defeated
death has paths not explored
and its own peculiar justice

even while we are dying
though standing on our feet
united in weakness, in hardness
brothers in stone

the dead escape the circle
they rise again
smile in a strange silence

V

Marathon

in this three — or six — thousand years
so much has passed before our eyes
we see nothing any longer

but beyond memory
rises a sudden gleam
brings strange visions
visions stranger even than you

a napkin in a crib
a sheet in a tomb
among the still leaves of the pepper tree

we know so well our lot
looking this way and that
wandering among broken stones
searching among ruins
that were — perhaps — once our homes
trying to remember dates
and brave deeds done

will we be able . . .?

we have been bound
and scattered
have wrestled — so they say —
with unreal problems

lost: we found a road
losing itself among seabogs and marshes
and blind armies sinking in the saltlake of Marathon

will we be able —
it is expected of us
according to the rules —
will we be able
to die
properly?

VI

almond flowers

a little farther
see

the almond flowers
the stone sparkles
the wave breaks

a little farther
look
there . . . no
a little higher

VII

Acheron

here the works of the sea, the works of love end
here where we end let them remember
those who come after
when blood flows
darkening memory
let them not forget
the weak ones among the asphodels
the powerless dead
as the heads of the victims
turn to the darkness

we had nothing

we know

peace

South Wales Echo

for David Jones

He does what is done in many places
what he does other
> *he does after the mode*
of what has always been done.
What did he do other
> *recumbent at the garnished supper?*
What did he do yet other
> *riding the Axile Tree?*

> *The Anathemata*

Moving Towards the Southfacing Form

Voices Off

In

A Shadow Dance for Puppets on Stilts

SOUTH WALES ECHO

For

The Night Before All Souls' Day

Foreword

'A man in himself is a city, beginning, seeking, achieving and concluding his life in the ways which the various aspects of the city may embody . . .'

(William Carlos Williams: 'Paterson')

That a child, uncertain as children are of the boundaries of guilt and innocence, should in certain circumstances surrender to the sense of an invading darkness will occasion no surprise. That the darkness should establish itself as unchangingly central in the consciousness of the child and on into youth and maturity, that the uncertainty should remain unresolved, that for the man — even though perhaps one of a naturally sanguine disposition — the sun should remain centred in darkness . . . what then? Have we here entered the realm of the pathological? Yet to the man himself it may well seem that the boundaries between health and sickness are as uncertain as those between innocence and guilt.

However all this may be see the child — playing in his school playground, games broken into to chant in unison with his companions 'bonfire night, bonfire night . . .' and excited talk of coming fireworks and guy. The eyes are bright, the voice clear yet these things veil an inward quailing before the necessary return home through the winter nightfall. His way will take him by the long wall of the City Gaol and the slums of Adam's Down. And he knows — it is the talk of the City — that inside the Gaol are three men, of whom two are brothers, awaiting execution, condemned to death for murder. He believes — perhaps mistakenly, who knows? — yet he believes with his father and mother and many others in the City that one of the men is innocent. Was he not sitting, his hat beside him, in the Anchor at the time of the murder, before leaping up at the sound of police whistles to rush into the street and run towards the Castle? He has heard too that another of the men has become insane — and for the child there is a peculiar slant of horror in the story going round the City that this man's insanity grows from his knowledge of his companion's innocence.

So the child walks home through the darkening streets each evening in growing apprehension and dread. At first there is some comfort in the bells sounding faintly across the sky from his school church. Yet as the evenings pass it seems to him there is fear in the sound of the bells too, as, in remembrance of another death, another execution of three, they call to prayer.

He marks, on more than one evening, a woeful group moving at the pavement edges among the passers-by in City Road — an elderly man tremulously singing out of a gaunt countenance, a ragged girlchild holding out his cap beside him, a tall black man a little apart only occasionally attempting to join the singing. There is that about the haggard singer — an air of utter dereliction, a hint of the more than half crazy — that is never to fade from memory. 'All the riff-raff of the world collects in Tiger Bay': so the child has been warned. Who is the singer? Some veritable Ishmael — outcast and wanderer from the outer reaches of the world — drifting up from Tiger Bay even as another Ishmael might have turned up, derelict and half-crazy, at

81

some dingy sea-port after the sinking of the Pequod by the White Whale? With a ghostly Dagoo in tow? Some late-born Odysseus after dreadful chance — 'and I only am escaped alone to tell thee' — cast up at the mouth of the Taff to follow his small white-faced Nausicaa to the grim palace in her home-city? The child never sees him again yet always sees him; shadowed away in the background, glimpsed in the eyes of any man, for the most part but a sleep and a forgetting, at a moment of stress or remembrance. Sees him more especially inwardly present in all those around the singing fool — those who hurry by indifferent, mocking, jeering, worried, or compassionate.

In the mind of the child this trinity of threes becomes confusedly inter-related; later indistinguishably one. So at least memory with blurred edges symbolises in the mind of the man the initiation in the mind of the child of the still enduring darkness.

One may perhaps fancy — why should one not? — the presence among the crowds in the city streets, on the night before the execution, of a stranger — a man from another place — waiting and listening, pausing and observing, and as he watches he overhears snatches of conversation, words spoken or sung, voices too breaking in from the backward reaches of his own mind, from the remote past, from the future, senses unuttered pressures in those around him as part of the total complex of thoughts and feelings and reactions charging the atmosphere in that particular time and space. It is certain the child of our story sensed the presence of some such stranger — a stranger unknowing it may be of the things which had come to pass in the city in those days. Yet the child thought not: and in this writing attempts to re-echo the words the stranger heard.

The scene is outside the 'The Anchor' as evening moves on to closing time. Passages printed in italics are singing voices.

the day of the Lord is darkness . . . even very dark . . .
he maketh the day dark with night . . .

and God made a wind to pass over the earth

'What if this present were the world's last night?'

John Donne

late news

South Wales Echo

late night news

now get along home now Lizzie get along home
you'll catch your death of cold in this wind
this night is no night
for the likes of you to be out in

echo

echo

there's the paperboy there
can't you hear him?
get the Echo

old bones at the fort of Didius
where the seaway crosses the river
have no ears
muffled crushed under many tramplings
they hear no voices

hear the bells of St Peter's ringing

they received no provisions for the way
have long been deaf to bells
to braying mules to crackling flames
when the splashing wave hid the church
set where the streams empty
they heard no sound
when the northmen moved in the creek
they heard no prayer[1]

                    listen
                    the bells of St Peter's ringing
                    ringing to evening prayer

living men though short of time
have ears to hear . . . let them
listen to the praying of the bells

we can't hear you
the wind is snatching the words
right out of your mouth . . . besides
we're busy men with little time to spare
time is pressing
we must think of other things
of iron and coal and bank accounts
and then of course there's silicosis

                    aye ! it's the dust they say that does it

from the assumptions of the grex
good Lord deliver us
when two or three are gathered together
in the name of the grex
make yourself scarce Tom

listen to the bells
withering in the wind
you remember Huw how Tim [2]
laughed like a blasted drain
at the stuttering old man in the billiard hall
who found his tongue to say
he'd heard the dogs of Annwn barking
in Parc Wyllt

                    bet y march bet y guythur
                    bet y gugaun cletyfrut
                    anoeth bid bet y arthur [3]

86

bright spearpower declines to fibrin
all that maddens and torments
all muck in the lees
what felo de se in bedlam? . . . no
keep the old sumpety sarcage moving on the tump Tom
outwalk Uranus [4]
he's out in the dark and cold
but he's bigger and older than Lizzie

echo

echo

little Dai loves sheep
but Lord! he's terrified of dragons
there's Salvation Band down at the corner
playing Cwm Rhondda they are

a saint I said a saint you call 'im
'umble and meek you call 'im?
the umbug of 'ippo I call 'im
'is Jesus 'as a bloody great snout . . . like 'im
my Jesus is a snotty little tyke . . . like me
'e'd ave knocked me down for tuppence he would
                    my old man said follow the band
                    and don't you dare dilly dally on the way

eight frozen plutonian years
since the dark fell in spring sunlight
hidden still in blueblack fire the phœnix sings
of flashing ice and snow
frozen to the dark rock
and sparkling stone [5]

                    in time we're weary
                    aye! weary
                    even of the dead

it's a bitter wind the east wind . . . smells empty
Courage mes enfants le diable est mort
this night before cockcrow
dancing bones will be crushed
Nox est perpetua una dormienda
what no ears
for oblique hints from Tophet? [6]
let's all off to the hop lads

> and our Tudor Rose [7]
> our truest treasure
> our red red rose
> our dearworthy darling
> our Rose of Sharon
> and we'll dance a jig to the melody
> she so sweetly plays in tune

bubble up bubble up!
all got sixpence?

> *ain't it grand*
> *to be blumin' well dead*

and now I'll not be lost in a maze
this sparkling stone will mark my days

aye won it up the valleys
on a ticket in the raffle
for the cracked chapel bell
but 'e won't last long
'e'll soon be with Dai central-'eatin'
mutton for 'Arry the boxer [7]
it's the dust they say that does it
let's drop in at the Anchor

> *don't y'know my dear*
> *the only thing I'd like my dear*
> *is a little bit off the top*
> *a little bit off the top*

late news   echo   echo
          who is that calling
                    calling
                         calling

calling all down Adam's Down
and now I'll not be lost in a maze
this sparkling stone
will mark my days

let him call in vain

aye! Gentleman Jim the baby giant!
left 'is 'at at the Anchor
there's talk 'e may get off
but tomorrow they'll all three hang

                    down they'll drop
                    following the elephant
                    man-monster Merrick
                    with his broken neck[8]

one's gone clean daft they say
there's the paperboy there
get the Echo
see what the Echo says

                    old Adam's cold[9]
                    frozen still
                    staring south
                    from the Castle Gate

the guileful deceptions of God[10]
what man can escape them
by what sprightly leaping
leaps he beyond them
snared in his blindness
slips he the noose scatheless?

                    sunny Jim 'e was
                    unlucky Jim now

89

no tears for Priam?
even Achilles wept
what voice is this
echoing down the airwaves?

ἀλλ' ἐκδιδάσκει πάνθ' ὁ γηράσκων χρόνος.[11]

sightlesse he drownes
againe he strides the blast
in teares teares teares

echo   echo

eyes darkened at Plwcca halog
sockets emptied at Cae budr
smoked out at the end of the way
        at Crwys Bychan [12]

bonfire night bonfire night
three little angels dressed in white

hush children
just been down Adam's Street
seeing Mary Anne . . . she said quietlike
tomorrow is All Souls' Day
so still and small she was
watching the candleflame
they've sent for the priest . . . she's expecting too
now come along home children its time for bed
come along home to Daddy Howe's down Sapphire Street [7]
and I'll tell you the story of Jack the Giantkiller
yes . . . and of blessed Michael the darkangel

bonfire night bonfire night
three little angels dressed in white

only a penny for the guy mister
not tuppence

not tuppence? are prices down then?
what matters tuppence or two and tuppence
Rawlins flung out his nets along the mudbanks
pulled out fish along the river
then . . . eyes thinned
forsook his nets and
proved combustible
outcapped Capper
at four and fourpence
what matter rising prices?
we the townsfolk meet the cost
we the indwellers pay the piper [13]

I too am under orders
to carry provisions for the way
down Adam's Street down Adam's Down
poor Mary Anne . . . and a child in her womb
a wild night this for men at sea
in the morning the crowd will be waiting at the wall
staring at the wall
the wall without windows
save us from eternal death
save us from eternal death
in that day . . . dies illa

                    dies irae

                    dona nobis pacem

nights I dream
all ways lots of people about
out somewhere and
lost voices calling all ways
lost in a dream
no way home

                    much will be well
                    much manner of thing will be well
                    Roland's horn will be heard [xb]
                    and grief-harbour's joy shall touch them

                              at the time I'll be easy
                              I'll say quietlike
                              well lads its time take it quietly
                              come on lads its time

waiting
            the lightning
                        the silence
                                    the thunder
                                                across Mockery Gap[14]

fire burns
wind blows
sun flames
thunder claps
and death comes on at last

                              He hurls the dark

lux est perpetua una
give us rest
let light shine
fallen fallen light renew

                              who'll head Corpus Christi[15]
                              to the Keeper at the Gate?

freezing the black fire burns
ringed in threefold fire[16]
the iceberg splashes the northern lights
astream to the bear and turning pole
gannet plunges

                              babble on Bert babble on
                              babble on in air

the day is dark
the wind has blown the sun
right out of the sky
but one more ancient than the sun
fireborn bright from the ancient waters
walks down Adam's Down tonight
                              echo
                                    echo
                                          late night news
            *   *   *   *   *
                        92

the bright   the utter   the still
      we utter

bright
    beyond bright
        beyond bright

utter
    beyond utter
        beyond utter

still
    beyond still
        beyond still

    blue-winged
    flashing
  flashing snowfire
    we utter

קָדוֹשׁ קָדוֹשׁ קָדוֹשׁ

beyond bright

    beyond utter

        beyond still

*   *   *   *   *

echo   echo

mae bys Mari Ann wedi brifo
A Dafydd y gwas ddim yn iach
Maer baban yn y cryd yn crio
A'r gath wedi crafu Joni bach [18]

there goes **Tom** again
singing for his supper
wonder where he comes from

sospan fach yn berwi ar y tan
sospan fawr yn berwi ar y llawr
a'r gath wedi crafu Joni bach [19]

'e's a regular queer plain scatty
doesn't know 'oo 'e is
and the whitefaced kid with staring eyes
white as chalk she is always with 'im
dosses down Tyger Bay with Omed 'amed
'e's big enough to knock spots off Jack Johnson [20]
look at 'im black as the ace of spades 'e is
should 'av been born in a rainstorm

'e's coming 'e's coming
'is 'ead is bended low
I 'ear them angel voices calling
    poor old Tom
        poor old Tom
            poor old Tom

Tom?
who the devil's **Tom**?

Tom?
Tom's **Tom** mister

who I am or what I am
who knows or cares
call me Ishmael . . . or Ulysses
he that poured libations to all the dead
come stormdriven back from that hateful stream
where powerless heads throng to the dark blood

flotsam I come
as to a place much longed for
as to one much prayed to
to the place where the streams empty
but I knew Tom of old . . . long ago
far back in the storm of the world-flow
he foresuffered all
humped trembling over Esau
bent in flamelight over Tilphussa's spring
gulped the black water
all worlds consumed in everliving fire
And eyeless under Suhir
sang with Shiddeh his bahilowi [21]

> *three blind mice three blind mice*
> *see how they run see how they run*
> *they all . . .*

there's tricky Tom Dolittle the artful dodger
in port after stormie seas
rejoycing with Sinbad the Sailor
Darkinbad sailing the Brightdayler
Rudolf Steiner on Pen-maen-mawr [22]

> echo   echo

the valley spirit never dies
take Tom now old Tom Mope-along
he's the joker in the pack
always rummaging in the dark
groping in odd corners
grumbling to himself things get lost
harking back
to old unhappy far-off things
things far away and long ago

Tom mooches south at sunrise
through the valley where the horses graze
heading for the northfacing form
lefthand touched by the brightshiner
he stills to the instant and sees
Alpha of the Cross invisible in light
but tiring
forgets
and nodding to the turn
lefthand shadowed slantwise crosses the stubble plough
edging the wood to Basho's pool [23]
dwinges muttering
babbles at the bear and turning pole
centres to the zodiacal light
faint foolscap glimmer

          Hyades rising Jupiter setting
          among the constellations of the heart

glances askance at the brightshiner
rising in the east [24]
and mumbles

    don't you remember you said
    he'd feed us
    all jetsam from worldstorm
    and lead us
    and cracked skulls and rags
    and crushed bones will dance

then slopes off north
to the breaking of the bread

        and turtle soup

       *   *   *   *   *

echo   echo

ἀλλ᾽ ἐκδιδάσκει πάνθ᾽ ὁ γηράσκων χρόνος.

Diawl Dai let's get home
this wind's whipping savage
right across the tidefields
enough to freeze the balls off a brass monkey
God help us all every manjack of us

      blow up seawind along Paumanok's shore

I woke up in the dark last night
thinking

      on every side
      in the flaring dark
      the paths tangle
      beyond ken to scan

going to the incinerator
it started to cry

      old nobodaddy's kid

      O ma ga ma ga
      O pa gas pie zoo [25]

please put a penny in the old man's hat
and he'll sing a song of

      O I'm a sorrowful
        sorrowful
        very sorrowful
          sweet fanny adams

move along there move along
the world's on the move

      death is now the phœnix nest
      and the turtle's

any bits or pieces
any silver
come on mister
you've the look of a stranger
let's divide by thirty
sixpence for all souls eh? [26]
look at all the lights in the windows
look

eyes in the wind
eyes in the wind down Adam's Down
                        down Adam's Down
                                    down Adam's
                                            down

all right Lizzie

                        Mae bys Mari Ann wedi gwella
                        A Dafydd y gwas yn ei fedd
                        Mae'r babi yny crud wedi tyfu
                        Mae'r babi yn y crud wedi tyfu
                        A'r gath wedi huno mewn hedd [27]

this night is no night
fire born from the bright the ancient waters
burns down Adam's Down tonight [28]

                        hurry along there hurry along

but hurrying men have ears to hear
bells in the wind ringing
voices praying in the wind
voices failing in the wind
voices in the wind singing

                        sospan fawr yn berwi ar y tan
                        sospan fach yn berwi ar y llawr
                        a'r gath wedi crafu Joni bach O
                        Dai bach y sowjur Dai bach y sowjur
                        Dai bach y sowjur a chwt igrys e
                                                mas [29]

time now lads come on lads its time

98

          echo
              echo
                  late night news

white to red
along the wall
the crosses blaze

            get along there get along
            the world's at the crack

won't you put a penny in the old bloke's hat?

          echo
            echo

London's burning London's burning
look yonder look yonder

           fire   fire
               fire
                  fire

O bring me some water

        koax

Ω meg gimme the clock gimme the clock[30]
no no put it back gimme Alph's button

          that scream
              that nameless unimaginable thing
                  out there

Judy judy judy jud ju ju ju d

     koax[31]

THE WIND BLOWS ON IN THE DARKNESS
INCREASING TO GALEFORCE LATER
YOU HEAR THE SOUND OF IT

        * * * * *

[Children's voices
  very
  softly
  pp]

blow wind blow wind blow
blow from the sea to this seagirt land
blow wind blow wind blow

                brekekekex

[Women's voices
  p]

blow wind blow wind blow
blow from the moon to this moonlit land
blow wind blow wind blow

                brekekekex koax

[Men's voices
  f]

blow wind blow wind blow
blow from the stars to this starlit land
blow wind blow wind blow

                brekekekex koax koax

[all souls
  ff]

blow wind blow wind blow
    blow from the dark [32]
    blow from the dark
    blow from the dark
blow wind blow wind blow
    blow blow blow

                koax

NIGHT NOW
ALL WAYS LOST NOW
NIGHT NOW NIGHT NIGHT
NIGHT DOWN ADAM'S DOWN

NIGHT

AND NIGHTLIGHT GLOW

Notes

A certain familiarity with the history of Cardiff as far back as Roman times is assumed.

A number of echoes from other writings are integrated into the substance of the work. If these are read in their original contexts they provide any comment necessary for fuller understanding. Peter Finch, the only living poet whose work I have consciously used in this way, has generously given me permission so to use it. Friends have drawn my attention to some passages that seemed to them obscure. In this connection the following notes may be helpful.

Among the Somali a man under extreme nervous mental or spiritual stress may seek help by calling his friends and womenfolk to a 'bahilowi'. They all meet at night in the open away from dwelling places and stand round him in a circle. He gives utterance to his suffering perplexity in a questioning chant. The others reply – sometimes singly, sometimes in unison – with comments, admonitions and exhortations accompanied by singing, clapping, and stamping.

A Somali – an old seaman who, when I knew him, had long been back in his own country – once told me how years before he had found himself stranded for a time in Tiger Bay. Friendless and in distress he had solaced himself one night by walking out onto a piece of waste land and holding a 'bahilowi' – pretending some of his people were present. He had been, he said, 'made whole' in this way. This lonely 'bahilowi' seems to have been held somewhere in the desolate area I often played in as a child – and knew as 'the tidefields'.

South Wales Echo might perhaps best be undestood as the result of a similar attempt to recover wholeness.

To the many ghostly friends
whose voices sound in the circle
an expression of gratitude is due :
more especially to Smart, Blake, Clare
and Tom O'Bedlam :

> *I knowe more than Apollo*
> *for oft when hee ly's sleeping*
> *I see the starres att bloudie warres*
> *in the wounded welkin weeping.*

1. Throughout the 8th and 9th centuries A.D. the prayer 'from the fury of the Northman deliver us' was commonly included in the litanies of the Church along the coastal regions of north-west Europe.

2. I remember walking with Huw Menai from Coity over the hill past Parc Wyllt. There we were glimpsed from within, over a wall, by a group of women standing among trees. They greeted us with a wild outcry: clamorously babbling, laughing and screaming: 'For upon all had come grief that might not be borne'. Huw started talking of the Dogs of Annwn. His formidable presence has been constantly with me in this attempt to restate our theme that afternoon as we talked the sun down the sky.

3. 'a grave for Mark, a grave for Gwythur
   a grave for Gugaun of the ruddy sword
   not wise (the thought) a grave for Arthur'
                          The Black Book of Carmarthen
                          Trans. Sir John Rhys.
the Arthur of Preiddeu Annwn, 'Arcturus': 'the Watcher of the North'. In Celtic Myth 'the wild land of hell' lies, frozen and dark, to the north.

4. During one revolution of Uranus earthborne Tom might circle the sun fourscore odd times even as Uranus achieves all but three completions of his orbit in one plutonian year. Each instant in all such gripped circlings within the structured order of the cosmos holds hidden within itself an end and a beginning: all the possibilities of a death and a birth into... but to step outside these circles, to follow Tom on this walk, one must needs buy stout boots — such as were stitched by Master Jacob at Gorlitz.
   See also Fludd's geocentric picture of the universe reproduced by Otto R Frisch on page 11 of his work *The Nature of Matter*.

5. 'this stone is sparkling white and red like a flame of fire . . . a flawless mirror in which all things live . . .' see *The book of the Sparkling Stone* by Jan van Ruysbroeck, chapter 4.
   Compare also *Ezekiel* 10:1; *Isaiah* 54:11.
   'in dense darkness thy stainless beauty sparkles'. Hindu *Hymn to The Destroyer.*

6. Tophet: 'the beating of the drum'.
   'and this, as they say, was the manner of sacrificing in Tophet . . . The statue of Moloch was of brass, hollow within, with its arms extended, and stooping a little forward. They lighted a great fire within the statue, and another before it. They put upon its arms the child they intended to sacrifice, which soon fell into the fire at the foot of the statue, putting forth cries . . . To stifle the noise of these cries they made a great rattling of drums, that the spectators might not be moved with compassion . . .'
                          Cruden's Concordance.

7. *Tudor Rose* – a popular streetgirl
   Dai central-'eatin' – the Devil
   'Arry the boxer – the undertaker.
Such humorous sobriquets are common in Wales.
   Daddy Howe: an old man. Well known for his kindness and integrity. He received into his home several orphaned children. (See also *Exodus* 24: 10).

8. See *The Elephant Man and other Reminiscences* by Sir Frederick Treves 1923. (T L S 9th June, 1972 page 655). Merrick known as the Elephant Man lived by exhibiting himself at freak shows – 'tuppence a time'. He is described as 'the most disgusting specimen of humanity ... a frightful creature that could only have been possible in a nightmare... There emanated from him a sickening stench... what made his fungoid deformity perhaps even more appalling were those portions of the body not invaded : the left ear perfect, the left arm and shoulder delicate as a woman's, the genitalia normal as any man's ... his only idea of happiness was to creep into the dark and hide ... he was a gentle affectionate and lovable creature free from any trace of resentment ... the weight of his head was so great that he could only sleep by raising his knees and resting his head against them...'

He often told Sir Frederick Treves the surgeon who befriended him in the last years of his life that he wished he could lie down 'like other people'.

One afternoon, in April 1890, he was found lying back on his pillow 'like other people'. He was dead – his neck broken by the weight of his head.

8b. The sentence on John Rowland one of the brothers convicted of murder was commuted shortly before execution to detention at His Majesty's pleasure in Broadmoor.

9. *old Adam's cold*
an early keeper at the Castle Gate was named Adam. He acquired landrights on the East Moor which lay between the 'warths' or tidefields along the Severn Estuary and the Castle. He sent his sons to herd his cattle and swine on the moor which became known as Adam's Down.

This Adam became indentified in my imagination with the First Adam.

10. a multitude of men of all nations has passed the point of no return. Then silence. In deepening anguish and despair after long waiting those left behind join in prayer for tidings : see the opening chorus of elders in Aeschylus' *The Persians* (lines 107-114).

11. 'but ever-ageing time teaches all things'. (See *Prometheus Bound* trans. Weir-Smyth, lines 980-983). Plotinus, who accepted the possibility of re-incarnation, in speaking of 'the sorrows of Priam' (Enneads 1 : 4) echoes the taunt of Hermes to Prometheus : 'alas? that is a word unknown to Zeus.' 'the one and only transmigrant is the Supreme Spirit' (Shankara). Plotinus shared this view.

12. public executions were carried out for many years at Crwys Bychan : the Little Cross in Cae budr : 'the defiled field'. The area was known as Plwcca halog : 'place of pollution'. Here the way from the north entered the town to run along the old Castle Road to the Big Cross. There it joined the ancient via maritima and swung west to cross the river beyond the south wall of the Castle. Before the Castle Gate another way branched south along St Mary's Street to the mouth of the river and the Church which was swept away by a tidal wave in 1607.

From early times these crossing ways carried the flows of human movement towards and away from the Castle. To venture too far from a stronghold brings danger. Men sailing from the estuary in the *Nova Terra* would, after a long voyage, come to a cold end under the shining of the Southern Cross : a constellation hidden below the horizons of their northern latitudes. And many an ocean-wanderer moving north under the ever-circling, ever-watchful, southward-gazing Bear reached an end likewise 'without fire, without bed.' Yet midgetina movements between the river-mouth and Castle – an impatient turning from his nets, or a careless running away from his hat – might initiate for a man, whether with or without fire, even darker farings.

13. Rawlins White, a fisherman from the Estuary, was burned at the stake before the Castle Gate in the reign of Mary under the revived statute *de heretico comburendo*.

Richard Capper suffered some years earlier.

The sheriff recorded the cost of the burning to the townsfolk at four and fourpence. A century earlier ropes for public hanging close to the present site of the Blue Anchor were priced at two pence.

14. Compare *Matthew* 24: 27.
Mockery gap: refers to the yawning gap of 'Chaos'
which came into being on the separation of heaven and earth:
see Hesiod's *Theogony* line 116 foll.

15. at this time in Cardiff, each year at the Feast of Corpus Christi, processions of children would converge from all quarters of the city at the south end of St Mary's Street and walk up to the Castle Gate – there to enter the Castle grounds and receive the Eucharistic Blessing. Doubtless for this reason some hint of the numinous attached itself for me to the way up to the Gate, and the endless coming and going of people there shared in the significance of these processions.

I remember, as a child, late one evening becoming – in some way I cannot now account for –lost among the ever-moving crowds in St Mary's Street. I was caught up among those strange anonymously hurrying crowds – crowds hurrying, as it seemed to me, nowhere . . . with growing inward panic I hurried too – hoping to reach the Castle : a central and known thing. The street then was to me endless. I did not reach the Castle and after some time I thought despairingly I was moving in the wrong direction. At that I turned and ran back and again failed to reach it. In this way I ran to and fro several times. Gripped by a sense of nightmare I could not ask for help . . . at last tears caught the attention of a friendly stranger who quickly pressed a sixpence into my hand and saw me safely on to a tramcar for home.

It was with a shock of strangely significant repetition that years later I read Dostoievsky's account of his encounter with the child in the Haymarket.

16. *ringed in threefold fire*
in the Christian tradition : baptismal, pentecostal, apocalyptic.

From the point of view of another tradition light will be thrown on this passage by reference to the translations from the Rigveda and notes in Macdonell's Vedic Reader. Of more especial interest are the hymns to Agni, Apam napat, and the Funeral Hymn.

Agni, the Sacred Fire burning at the heart of all the worlds appears as threefold light in the beggar at evening to command Ratri, Night, to 'bring the world to rest'. One of the functions of Agni, who is born of the celestial waters and appears in the east, 'clothed in lightning', 'widely shining forth to all men', is to conduct the dead by the paths of the ancestors to the highest heaven, where they are united to bodies 'free from disease and frailties, complete and without imperfections'.

16b. A friendly aside to two distinguished contemporary British philosophers.

17. Compare *Isaiah* 6: 3.
One thinks too of the music heard by Boehme 'shortly after midnight' on November 21st, 1624.

18. *Mae bys Mari Ann wedi brifo –*
    Mary Anne's finger is cut
    David is not well
    the baby is crying in the cradle
    and puss has scratched little Johnny

19. *sospan fach yn berwi ar y llawr –*
    the small saucepan is on the fire
    the big one on the hob
    and puss has scratched little Johnny . . .

20. During this period Jack Johnson, the great American Negro boxer, (at one time heavyweight champion of the world) was held in high honour in South Wales.

21.   the Somali name Shiddeh means 'born in pain'

Shiddeh sings under Suhir – the star Sirius – believed to exert a baneful influence. See Jacob Boehme *Signatura Rerum* chapter xvi 'on the weeping of Adam in Esau.'

22. Steiner spoke at Pen-maen-mawr of gigantic elemental presences locked up in the planetary structures under his feet.

23. *Basho's pool*
Suzuki in his commentary on the Lankavatra Sutra speaks of the shadow dance as 'reflected on a screen of eternal solitude and tranquillity . . .'

    the Mahayanist eye is always gazing at the screen itself . . .'

The whole passage from which these words are taken will be found one of intense interest for our theme . . . but for Tom a sudden flaming word has, more decisively than for Yeats at the crossways, broken into the ancient reverie.

24.   Compare *Revelation* 7:2. The Catholic Requiem Mass for the Dead.

25. 'O mother earth, mother earth,
      O Father, Son of Earth, Zeus'
compare Aeschylus' *The Suppliant Maidens* lines 885-901.

26. *sixpence for all souls*
Compare Dostoievsky's account of his visit to the Haymarket in 1862 : 'In the Haymarket . . . I saw a girl of about six, no older, all in rags . . . no one paid any attention to her . . . she walked along with a look of such sorrow, such hopeless despair . . . she kept shaking her head from side to side as if discussing something . . . I offered her sixpence. She took the silver coin, then shyly with timid amazement, looked me in the eyes and suddenly took to her heels, as if afraid I would take the money back from her.' (See also *Luke* 24:18).

27. Mary Anne's finger is better
    David is in his grave
    the baby in the cradle has grown
    the baby in the cradle has grown
    and puss is asleep . . .

28. Heraclitus : 'fire when it has advanced will judge and convict all things'.
c.f. Heraclitus Fragments xx; xxii; and xxvi
πῦρ ἀείζωον: an infinite eternal self-creating substance . . . differentiating itself into the returning movement of the many to itself . . . Isaiah: 'The shining of a flaming fire by night'.

29. Voices singing in chorus from inside 'The Anchor'.

> 'the big pot is boiling on the fire
> the little one on the hob
> and puss has scratched little Johnny again
> O little Dai the soldier
> little Dai the soldier
> little Dai the soldier
> Look ! the tail of his shirt is out . . .'

Compare the pair Dadeni or 'Cauldron of Rebirth'

30. the prototypes of Punch and Judy have been seen as – in an old mystery play – Pontius Pilate and Judas. See Revelation 21:6.

31. the ghosts of vivisected frogs respond in chorus from the underworld. Compare Aristophanes' *The Frogs* in which the frogs croak in time to the oarstrokes of Dionysus as he rows perforce across to Hades : croaking 'faster faster' . . .

32. the dark beyond the stars : ungrund equally to both Great Bear and Southern Cross.

Compare Aeschylus' *Seven against Thebes* lines 854-860

> 'as you sigh dear friends
> as you weep
> beat with your hands
> oarstrokes in the wind across Acheron
> speeding the black ship unknown to Apollo
> unknown to the sunlight
> to the dark shore
> that welcomes all'

The Shield of Achilles

for Louise de Bruin

μή πως δείσει᾽ ἐνὶ θυμῷ·

Iliad 24:672

.

The reflection of the uncreated in the created necessarily presents itself under diverse aspects, and even under an indefinite variety of aspects, each of which has about it something whole and total, so that there are a multiplicity of visions of the cosmos, all equally possible and legitimate in so far as they spring from the universal and immutable principles.

Titus Burkhardt

To every shield, there is another side, hidden.

A. N. Whitehead

In the Hesiodic account of the world-ages, preserved in the ancient writing known to us as the 'Works and Days', the poet briefly describes the age of the heroes. He tells us that the heroes were 'nobler far' than their immediate predecessors and in this they reversed for a time the downward drift of history to degeneration that he has been describing. The heroes reflected in their natures something of the integral wholeness of men in the Golden Age. It was as though for a moment the river of time flowed back on itself in brief eddies, caught up in memories of its source. And this act of remembrance wrought, as all such acts of remembrance do, happier destinies for many men than had been the common lot of those born into the age that had just passed away. For these earlier men of bronze, men insatiate of war and violence, had destroyed each other and gone down into Hades — 'terrible though they were, black death seized them: they passed from the light of the sun and left no name'.

Then:

> 'The Son of Cronos made yet another race of men to live on the bounteous earth, and these were godlike men — a race of heroes. Many died in grim battle fighting for the flocks of Oedipus around seven-gated Thebe . . . yet others, sailing over the great gulf of the sea to Troy, perished for fair-haired Helen's sake. There death hid them. But to the rest Zeus, the Father of gods and men, gave a dwelling at the ends of the earth, where free from all care they live on the Islands of the Blessed in deep-eddying Ocean . . . there untouched by sorrow, those happy heroes dwell . . . and Cronos rules over them . . .'

The heroes were men born into a world disrupted by the violence of the Age of Bronze, and were necessarily warriors — yet warriors who were never forgetful of the gods that are forever; men who 'lifted up their hands in prayer to the broad heavens', and prayed 'that war and strife might cease from among men'. They were men for the most part simple, passionate, unreflecting. Their virtues were the virtues of warriors — truthfulness and courage. Their vision of the world was the vision of the warrior — 'God is day and night, winter and summer, war and peace, surfeit and hunger . . .' 'War is father of all, king of all; some he makes gods, some men; some bond some free . . .' 'The name of the bow is life: its work is death . . .' Such are some of the utterances of Heraclitus: the philosopher who saw most deeply into the heart of the hero. We shall have occasion in what follows to recall more than once other of the fragmented sayings of Heraclitus that have come down to us.

In this world of war and peace, amid the issues of slavery and freedom a man's character is his fate. The hero is the man who works out his destiny centring, in truth and courage, to the fiery element in his own soul: for this fiery element in his soul is the

111

reflection of the divine creative fire that brings the worlds into being. In battle the body of the hero is protected by his shield. And his soul is protected by that which his shield symbolizes — the totality of his world vision. In seeking in some degree to share this vision we may turn to the description given in Homer, towards the end of the eighteenth book of the Iliad, of the forging of the Shield of Achilles.

The shield is wrought out of the elemental metals — gold, silver, bronze and tin — by the divine artificer Hephaestus, the God of Fire. Even so the cosmos is wrought by the ever-living divine fire eternally differentiating itself into the many, and the never-ending returning movement of the many to itself. This cosmic process of return out of the conflicts of the many and the restoration demanded by Justice, of equilibrium at the source, is war issuing in peace. The ever-living fire centred in itself beyond all worlds lies at the heart of all worlds: from it flow all movement, all life, all knowledge. It is the Eternal: 'that which never sets', that which at the end of each world-age destroys the old and kindles the new. It may be truthfully called by other names such as Zeus, justice, wisdom, logos. It is both willing and unwilling to be so called. Willing in that such names reflect qualities in its nature: unwilling in that in essence it lies beyond all such qualities. This divine fire forges into existence the structured cosmos.

The cosmos is imaged by the Homeric warrior to himself as a sphere. Across the horizontal diametrical plane stretches the flat disc of the earth encircled by the vast streams of Oceanus — ever flowing back into itself. The earth is covered by the inverted bowl of the overworld — a bronze[1] dome across which the sun, moon, and stars move in their risings out of Oceanus in the east, to their settings into Oceanus in the west. Earth rests on the underworld of Erebos and Hades rooted at its greatest depth in the gulfs of Tartarus. About the upper hemisphere of the overworld glitters the threefold light of the Empyrean. The brazen walls of Tartarus are enclosed by threefold darkening layers of night. The cosmic sphere is held in an outer wheel of darkness and light which in its rotations reflects into the cosmos the cycles of birth and death at all levels of existence, from that of the cosmos itself to all that comes to be within it. 'For the same cause that brings us out into the light of the sun, brings on dark Hades too.' Within the circle of the earth the individual souls move at death to the streams of Oceanus whence they gravitate down into the underworld to emerge into new states within the earth-cycle — or, after a sojourn in the Islands of the Blessed, may be attracted up into the overworld and on into the Empyrean; that is, to a state of being beyond the circles of the cosmos.

These journeyings of the soul are conditioned by its nature as a reflection of the divine fire. 'Of soul thou shalt never find boundaries, not though thou trackest it on every path; so deep is its cause . . .' For its cause is one with the ever-living fire itself. So the hero lives and dies seeking to preserve his soulfire unquenched, to return at death beyond the circles of the cosmic fires to the ever-living divine fire: the one source and end of all. His living seeks to be a continual act of remembrance of his source: an awakening from the sleep of forgetting, from the death of utter forgetting. And his dying, as return to source, is symbolized in his deathrite of immolation by fire.

In some such sort as this is the vision of the cosmos that served to protect and shield the soul of the Homeric hero and to preserve it into eternal life. And of this the Shield of Achilles as forged by Hephaestus is the symbol both in what it emphasizes and in what it omits.[2] The wrought shield in its structures holds no black iron. For the soul of

[1] Bronze: the third transmutation, as the world-ages unfold, of the Empyrean fire into the containing hemispheres of the cosmos. The cosmos as such cannot be other than limited and shaped.

[2] The Shield of Achilles may be compared in this respect with the Hesiodic Shield of Heracles in which the figure of Fear stands staring from the centre: a reflection of the Age of Bronze in the full tide of its cruelty and violence. In the 'Iliad' the coming Iron Age is fore-shadowed by the iron tip of the arrow of Pandaros launched in violation of a sacred oath. Iliad Bk. 4, Line 123. This is the only occasion in which Homer describes an arrow or spearhead as 'made of iron'.

Achilles is not destined to face the deadening weight of the age yet to come. His shield is made of gold and silver, of bronze and tin, for it must hold within itself, structured into protective shape, all the metallic influences inhering in the cosmic process up to and including the age in which he himself lives. Omitted too from the shield is any representation of the underworld. The attention of the hero is to be directed to and concentrated on the earth wherein he is to work out his destiny, and to the overworld to which he aspires.

And what aspects of the world are imaged on the shield for the acceptance and delight and protection of the warrior? The broad earth itself: and over the earth the circlings of the unwearied sun, the moon at the full, and the constellations across the heavens. And, under these high presences, the cities of men wherein are marriages and torchlit feastings and dance and song. And the fields of men wherein are ploughing and seedtime and harvest and vineyards and honey-sweet wine and summer departing before approaching winter to the sounding lyre and the delicate voices of boys singing the Linos-song. The ways of peace.

But the paths of war also; men and dogs poised in a threatening circle around lions devouring a bull; ambushed youths slain as they play on their pipes among their cattle at the fords of swift-flowing rivers; women and children and old men at the walls of embattled cities.

And the protections of law — resolution of dissension in peace. The folk gathered to witness an issue of homicide and the mode of settlement — old men sitting on polished stones in a circle that images the circles of the cosmos, and rising to speak in turn — the staves in their hands recalling, to the remembrance of all who are present, Hermes the messenger of Zeus — as they seek fair judgement.

For all these things, the works and days of men on the earth, the shield as forged by Hephaestus for Achilles, enjoins a certain joyful acceptance — an acceptance of the natural order of things under heaven: an order arising from the attunement of opposite tensions as of the bow or the lyre.

And around earth — 'around the uttermost rim of the strongly wrought shield' — flows the ever-circling divine river Oceanus. Flows from its source at the risings of the sun: thalean[3] water from the ever-living fire. Oceanus the begetter of all becomings initiator of all destructions, the generating waters of all possibilities flowing in the twilight where the down-reflected light of the overworld meets the upcast shadow and dark of the underworld. Oceanus: that unfathomably strange river into whose waters we cannot step twice for other waters are ever flowing on to us, in whose waters we both are and are not; waters flowing in that circle wherein every point on the circumference is at once an end and a beginning, a forgetting, a remembrance and a regeneration.

Such was the Shield Hephaestus forged and laid at the feet of Thetis, the mother of Achilles. 'And like a falcon she swooped down from snowy Olympus' bearing it to her son. She finds him weeping beside the body of Patroclus. The black fires of Tartarus burning in the soul of Achilles have incurred retribution. He has sinned against justice, against the divine fire in his own soul. He has prayed that his own comrades suffer defeat in battle. He has brought bitter sorrow to himself and to his people. Now he is defenceless in soul and body. He has lost his armour to Hector: the armour given by the gods to his father. And Patroclus is dead.

Every man in every age — be it of gold or silver or bronze or iron — bears within himself the potentialities of all the ages. Any man may at any time turn his eyes back to the source. The virtues of the hero — truthfulness and courage — effect creative and

---

[3] The thalean waters: the 'chaotic' waters flowing in the void separating the overworld and underworld, out of which arises by crystallization the islanded Earth-disc.

redeeming transfigurations in all situations, in all wars both outer and inner, both visible and invisible. In his dereliction, Achilles — the man of war — prays 'that war and strife may cease'. He wills to return to source. But on his return he must follow the paths of his destiny. His pyre can only be kindled by the funeral fires of Patroclus and Hector. For Achilles is fated to die in battle himself as soon as he has slain Hector: even as Hector in the slaying of Patroclus brings on his own death at the hands of Achilles. So now for Achilles his acceptance of the Shield involves his acceptance of his own death in the near future fighting at the Scaen Gate. The Shield will protect him until his fated death which is yet self-chosen. He chooses the fiery death of the warrior rather than to live on into old age — for 'greater dooms win greater destinies' in a world where all movement is the movement of the one ever-living fire in all its transformations dying into rebirths — where life is not broken by death but perpetually renewed. So Achilles, the grief of the people, accepts the Shield and moves along the paths of return.

'The paths of return'. And with the return compassion will flow once more in the heart of Achilles. In the presence of Priam, as the old man stretches out his hands in supplication to the face of the man who has slain his sons, there enters into the heart of Achilles the desire for weeping — and he lifts up the old man by his hand and weeps and speaks to him: 'Ah, unhappy man, many and terrible are the woes thou hast endured in thy soul . . . and now thou hast come alone to meet the eyes of him who has slain thy sons, so many and brave . . . and we hear that of old thou too wast happy and blest . . . but now ever around thy city are battles and slayings of men . . .'

And, towards the end of the Iliad, we glimpse Achilles once more. Having returned to Priam his dead son, he promises to hold up the fighting until the funeral fires have burnt the body of Hector. Then in farewell he clasps the old man's right hand at the wrist — 'lest he should know fear in his heart'.

A last gesture: of acceptance, reconciliation and final restitution.

For the purposes of this essay readers may be referred more especially to the eighteenth book of the Iliad: lines 462 to the end and Hesiod's 'Works and Days': lines 109–201.
The Fragments of Heraclitus have also been freely drawn upon.

Postscript

'waiting for the restitution of all things'

Acts 3:21

True Listening

for Judith Lang

τὸ πνεῦμα ὅπου θέλει πνεῖ, καὶ τὴν φωνὴν αὐτοῦ
ἀκούεις, ἀλλ' οὐκ οἶδας πόθεν ἔρχεται καὶ ποῦ ὑπάγει·

John 3:8

On the breaking of the Bread, Thou are not broken, nor art Thou divided.

St. Thomas Aquinas:
"Sermon of the Body of Our Lord"

Why is it that true listening is a faculty of only a few? Why is it that so often so-called dialogues are but a collection of monologues conducted with closed ears and hearts?

Henrik Kraemer:
"The Communication of the Christian Faith"

While not attempting to answer Kraemer's question in any full sense we would like to indicate some of the problems involved in our attempt as Christians to enter into fruitful dialogue with the scientific thought of the west and the metaphysical doctrines of the east. In this connection at least part of the answer to the question is to be found in the fact that many of us try to both speak and listen without any clear understanding as to what we mean by words like science, metaphysic, revelation, religion and many others. Much of the conflict in the world today between great historic cultures and traditions, and much of the difficulty of arriving at mutual understanding in depth arises from this cause. It would be fair comment to say that this is the case often even when eminent and deeply sincere authorities in various fields are engaged in the attempt to enter into true understanding. There is not rarely a fundamental lack of clarity in the use of words which results in a deepening confusion and inability to communicate. In many cases it seems as though the underlying structures of consciousness deny even the possibility of understanding modes of thinking and living and being alien to our own. Yet often this seeming incapacity arises from a defect of the will conditioned below the surface consciousness.

In what follows an attempt is made to clear away some of the misunderstandings that arise whenever we approach these problems. The purpose is to stimulate discussion while remaining if possible clear as to the meaning of the terms we are using.

This being so it is necessary to attempt definitions of some words fundamental to the discussion and to accept these definitions as valid at least within the framework of our present considerations.

1. Revelation is that which establishes in truth man's relation to that which transcends process.
2. Religion is the attempt to incorporate revelation in cultural and historical forms, i.e. in process.
3. Metaphysic is the attempt to arrive at knowledge of that which transcends process.
4. Science in its pure form, which is all we are here concerned with, is the attempt to arrive at knowledge of the laws governing process.

These definitions, though very generalised and abstract, are sufficient for our present purpose, and it is clear that if we accept them there is in principle no conflict between them. It is also clear that they involve each other in the sense that each needs the others to establish itself in its own fullness and integrity. This mutual need and interdependence is the necessary consequence of the presence in each case of what we have called "process", which is that in the structure of the world which is constantly changing. A complete and authentic tradition would be achieved by a balanced fusion of all four elements in which each remained true to itself without distorting the others. There are however in the world elements arising from the facts of process, freedom and evil which forever prevent this achievement "under heaven". Yet the necessity lies upon us always to be striving towards its realisation.

Certain consequences implicit in the definitions given above, when taken together as constituting a description of an authentic tradition considered in its totality, should be noted. Revelation — the Word — in its source prehuman and transcendent, and as such inaccessible without grace, which is an eternal outflow of divine creativity and mercy into the temporal world, is in principle both complete in itself, and that which enters into, completes and renders authentic our religious and metaphysical and scientific strivings. This means we must clearly recognise that revelation is present in all human activities in so far as they participate in truth at any level. In examining any particular traditional form, however, we become aware of certain distortions, certain impeding and negative elements, certain irruptions of evil.

The distortions will usually arise from a lack of balance induced in the form by the powerful influence of the central human tendency in the collectivity concerned. Thus we see in the eastern traditions the strong urge to pure metaphysical realisation has tended to weaken the other factors which are nevertheless present. We see in the modern west the striving towards scientific understanding and control of process resulting in an almost complete discounting of the metaphysical order, and a grave weakening of the religious culture. In ecclesiastical Christianity, as it took form in the middle ages, the religious cultus obscured the scientific perspective, at least at the level of general awareness. In Islam the emphasis on divine transcendence has made it difficult for Muslims to realise the divine immanence: to this the fate of al-Hallāj bears witness.

The impeding and negative elements present in all historic forms arise from the obscurity and weight of the human substance involved, and inhibiting historical, geographical and climatic factors.

The irruptions of evil break forth under the pressure of satanic forces present in the world which can by no means be discounted in the light of revelation or of history.

The point we are making here is that all historic forms without exception show such failures and ambiguities and all fall short of the glory of God.

Against this general background we now consider some of the implications of our understanding of revelation in relation to the great historic traditions of man. Revelation in so far as it is essentially and supremely that which establishes in truth man's relation to the transcendent is clearly manifested in all its divine fullness in Christ, the universal Man at once God-Man, Man-God. This is so because metaphysic and science as such are not in principle centred on man. Pure metaphysic seeks as it were to forget man in order to realise the transcendent, though in practice it is always forced to take man into account. Pure science likewise seeks to forget man except in so far as he is involved in process – for science is by its very nature centred upon achieving an understanding of process. If accepted these considerations force us to see in Christ the fullness of revelation. This will also mean that all religious forms are in fact centred on Christ whether manifest or "hidden", and can only be properly understood in the light of Christ. This will not mean that historic "Christian" forms are necessarily more filled with the spirit of Christ than others. Christ Himself infinitely transcends any and every historic form and all alike lie under His judgement and mercy. Yet in so far as Christianity is more consciously and decisively centred on Jesus of Nazareth the incarnate Christ, who as such reflects the Universal Man to all men through and beyond their cultural conditioning; it should and possibly does reflect His grace out into the world in a more abundant way than other religions. It should not need saying that this possibility in no way implies any cultural superiority in a "Christian" civilisation which is in fact very far from centred on Christ. There remains too the tragic paradox — and this is a fact never to be forgotten — that the manifest presence of Christ always attracts attack from the forces of evil in forms more intense and malignant than those assailing the "hidden" and universal presence of Christ in all human societies. Such demonic forces are not only a source of acute danger and suffering to the "non-Christian" world, but it may well be that only with the help of all the spiritual resources present in that world will the "Christian" world overcome the evil at work within itself. It may be also that only in accepting this help will we come to a true understanding of what the coming of Christ into the world means with all that it implies.

To turn next to the far eastern traditions. It cannot be too clearly understood that these traditions are centred on the metaphysical perspective and that in them the religious striving as such is subordinated to the metaphysical aim of pure knowledge of the transcendent. Yet to seek to understand these doctrines as rational speculative systems of thought comparable to the systems of western philosophers in which discursive reasoning processes play a predominant part, is to misunderstand their nature. The basic teachings are to be understood rather as descriptions of spiritual states arrived at as a result of highly developed disciplines and modes of contemplation, and such discursive reasoning as appears is a subordinate and secondary rationalisation of achieved states of consciousness. The basic striving underlying the techniques used is always in the direction of achieving an ever more radical exteriorization of and detachment from process, and the aim is to realise the pure subject underlying all process. To the radically objectified structure of consciousness of the majority of western men such an aim is so baffling as to approach for them something close to complete unintelligibility. This is indicated by the widespread and persistent attempt by many western thinkers, both philosophical and religious, to interpret oriental metaphysic as analagous to western mysticism. This attempt breaks down on the fact that this mysticism reveals an objectified structure of consciousness in accordance with the general objectification of the western mind in all its forms. The western mystic sees God as the "absolute" object and seeks union with God through modes of striving essentially devotional. The eastern sage seeks to realise the "absolute" subject through techniques of concentration and abstraction from process that are essentially intellectual. The faculty used is an intellectual intuition that increasingly divests itself of process and therefore cannot be identified even in a qualified sense with either discursive reasoning or devotional relationship. The contemplative intelligence seeking to realise within itself the eternity of the transcendent intellect is not surrendering itself to "individualism and arrogance". The pure subject is the transcendent, universal and divine intellect, and the individual in approaching it must needs rid himself of all notions he may have of any special value in himself as an individual. He is no more reasonably to be accused of "individualism and arrogance" than the man who wearying indoors walks out into the light of the sun. The basic difference in orientation between mystic and sage reveals itself clearly in the typical modes of expression used by say a mystic of the stature of Boehme as compared with those used by the Buddhist Nagarjune or the Hindu Shankara.

The state of consciousness achieved by the sage, or its value for the whole of the spiritual world within which he lives and moves and has his being, cannot be participated in, or understood or judged by men of alien traditions whose whole structure of consciousness would have to be, as it were, dismantled before they could even begin to move towards the possibility of sharing it in some remote degree. This being so, it would be wiser to suspend all attempts at judgements issuing in denials that such modes of spiritual striving can be a response to a true inward revelation comparable in value to objective revelation in history as understood in the Semitic traditions. The insistence of many Christian theologians that oriental traditions are purely immanent and are not related to any inner source of revelation or flow of grace can only arise from a misunderstanding or a perverse wilfulness. To speak in terms intelligible within the Christian tradition which should be acceptable to these theologians, it must be said that their judgements as to where and under what conditions the Holy Spirit can or cannot move are presumptuous and reveal a surprising lack of humility in the face of divine mysteries. Christ mediates grace through the Holy Spirit to all men when and where he wills to do so, and if He mediates it in ways unseen and through traditional forms strange to men nurtured in Semitic religious traditions, then let such men remember His words: "In my Father's house are many mansions"; "Other sheep I have which are not of this fold"; "The wind bloweth where it listeth, and thou hearest the sound thereof, but cans't not tell whence it cometh, and whither it goeth: so is everyone that is born of the Spirit". Christians also face offences and stones of stumbling in the way of Truth.

We will now consider the influence and meaning of science in so far as it penetrates sometimes as a disturbing and distorting factor and sometimes as a corrective factor to our general religious and cultural situation. Science in that it seeks a position of ever greater detachment from process in order to examine it with a cool and discerning eye remains an ever-necessary sanative influence in dispelling sentimentality and superstition. It strives to see the process as it is and refuses to be deflected by non-scientific presuppositions of any kind. This is all to the good and unless it remains present as an element in our thinking we are always liable to fall into subjective fantasies. This remains the greatest service science has rendered us. Unhappily however, the intense preoccupation of the scientific outlook with process increasingly induces an incapacity for either genuine metaphysical insight or religious response to revelation, which uncorrected leads to an extremely dangerous blindness and naïveté outside the purely scientific field. That a society predominantly in the grip of such limited thought-forms inevitably finds itself in acute danger and a state of threatening disintegration hardly needs stressing at the present time. In so far as the western world today reveals this extremely dangerous imbalance in its structures and strivings in favour of the scientific perspective — and it must be acknowledged this imbalance affects not only secular society but also and equally the religious tradition — then it is clear that the eastern metaphysical traditions could be for us the source of a much-needed corrective. In fact it is not too much to affirm that not until we accept this corrective will we attain to a true and sane understanding of the limitations of science and be in a position to deal with the dangers arising from its misuse. In connection with this necessity it is significant that some eminent scientific men are displaying an interest in and understanding of the eastern traditions which reveals an instinctive turning in the right direction for the corrective they need. Equally it is clear that many orientals have become acutely conscious of the distortions produced in their societies by their predominantly metaphysical bent and of the high price they have had to pay for this at the sociological level, and are consequently seeking to assimilate emphases from western traditions both scientific and religious which will help them achieve a truer balance.

In one direction — that of cosmology — both modern science and eastern metaphysical doctrines pose problems for Christian theology that have not yet in any profound sense been faced. Christian thinkers need to take more seriously the words of St. Paul: "For the invisible things of Him from the creation of the world are clearly seen, being understood by the things that are made, even His eternal power and Godhead". The customary evasive talk of one unique world with a beginning and an end neatly fitted to the notions of so many of our theologians in no way disposes of the multiplicity of worlds endlessly flowing from the infinite creativity of God. The truth is that this "one-unique-world" theology is more or less adequate only in a strictly limited sense as applied to this particular world of man on this planet and the Biblical revelation is a revelation to this particular world. To say this is not to deny the full divinity of Christ or the absolute validity of His revelation, for this revelation is at one with revelation as it must be to any possible world which cannot be other than centred on God through the second Person of the Trinity. In this matter Christian theology must sooner or later come to terms with a cyclical cosmology understood as the reflection in creation of the hidden inner infinities of the Godhead. "For the Spirit searcheth all things, yea, even the deep things of God."

Accepting the admonitions of the Divine Wisdom as it comes to us from the eighth chapter of the Book of Proverbs, and listening to the prophetic voice of Isaiah (more especially 25:6–8) and the echoes sounding centuries later on this theme in the New Testament — attending too, with all the depth of "attention" urged on us by Simone Weil, to the voices speaking to us out of religious traditions that lie beyond the circles of our own Christian tradition — it is open to us to root ourselves in manifold certainties.

That with God all things are possible is certain. That God wills the transfiguration of the whole creation and the salvation of all men within that creation is certain. That evil, even in its most radical and malignant manifestations can never be more than a fading shadow in the presence of God is certain. The Divine Name Jesus — God saves — tells us that man is saved by God and not by any system of beliefs he may hold about God: beliefs that in any case can never be more than inadequate before the mystery of God. This is an axiom of any sane theology. What extremes of cruelty and intolerance might have been avoided had it always been remembered. That there are precious veins of truth and insight in the "non-Christian" traditions of millions of our neighbours is as certain as that all truth wherever found is woven at once out of and back into the seamless garment of Christ. That we who live and die within the ambience of the Christian tradition stand in need of these insights and also of forgiveness for our many crimes and incomprehensions in the face of these neighbours is certain. We are entering a time in human history in which these truths can no longer be evaded as they have been all too often in the past. One certainty denied us is that we, who claim to speak in the name of the Biblical revelation, are always and infallibly right. The "I am" of Jesus before Abraham remains with no shadow of turning ever: after all the self-limiting ecclesiastical perspectives of history have left not a wrack behind.

Voices we can no longer be deaf to call to us from the past, from the future: echoing from beyond the limitations of our own cultural assumptions. Should we not open our minds and hearts and — stilled to utter attention — listen?

Surely even the few brief glances we have taken here at the problems before us reveal the need for true humility and true listening among us all whether we be scientists or theologians, western men or eastern men, unbelievers or Christians?

Christians especially must ever be open to receive the unsearchable riches of Christ's grace as revealed in the neighbour that lives outside the radiations of His grace as inwardly received through faith in the historic traditions of Christianity.

Appendix

with gratitude to Alan Clodd

An Introduction written by David Blamires for the first publication of *South Wales Echo* by the *Enitharmon Press* in 1973.

It is not often that one comes across a poem of the moving quality of *South Wales Echo*, and I count it a privilege to be asked to introduce it to a wider readership. Since first reading it and watching its development to final shape, I have delighted in its taut, allusive language and peculiarly compelling poetic strength. Even at a first reading it communicates a sense of power and starts to reverberate in one's mind. But it is only with subsequent re-readings that one begins to grasp at all adequately its real depth and complex texture. It is not an easy poem to read, but since it communicates something immediately before it is understood, one is all the time being spurred on to find out more, to search for the key to the allusions that one does not at first comprehend.

The poem focuses on an experience of the author's childhood, but it is an experience which must have been shared by many people at the time. The incident here recalled – of three men awaiting execution, one believed to be innocent and another become insane at the realization of this fact – is simple in outline, but has all the elements of a universal theme. At the symbolic season of All Souls' Night we are invited into an exploration of the mysteries of death and judgement. Not in the abstract, but in the particular setting of Cardiff in the early years of the twentieth century – Cardiff with St Peter's church and the Salvation Army band, the newspaper seller, the businessmen and the street gossip, Adam's Street, the Anchor pub, Tiger Bay and the mining valleys close at hand. Snatches of music-hall songs, *Sospan fach* and *Cwm Rhondda* mingle in the cold evening air. The whole poem is firmly anchored in the concrete details of the everyday. The city of Cardiff, evoked in all its particularity, is nonetheless all cities, and Adam's Down with the symbolism of its name, is the City of Man: a 'night city' lit up at the last by the 'nightlight glow' of the City of God.

At every moment, however, the present gathers up the past, whether in simple historical facts, in legend, or in telling words and phrases from as diverse sources as Homer and Whitman. The Roman fort of Didius gave the City its name, and the soldiers who are buried there near the *via maritima* connecting West Wales with Londinium are the first of the dead whose memory is invoked in the poem. The 'crackling flames' of this opening sequence recall, if only obscurely, the burning of Cardiff by Owain Glyndwr and the burning of heretics at the end of Crwys Road, a motif taken up again a few pages further on. The image of fire leads us to *London's burning* towards the conclusion of the poem. Such an intricate interlinking of themes is characteristic of the entire structure of *South Wales Echo*.

When furthermore we read of the legendary dogs of Annwn, the Welsh Hades, which figure in the story of Pwyll in the *Mabinogion* and have become part of Welsh traditional lore, they are juxtaposed in their uncanniness with the claim of the 'stuttering old man in the billiard hall' that he had heard them at Parc Wyllt, the South Wales lunatic asylum. References like this give a strong historical and literary resonance to the poem, though the matter does not end here. The scale of allusion extends to include the joyful confidence of Catullus whose *nox perpetua* of love is transmuted into the *lux perpetua* of the requiem mass. Then there are stark lines echoing from Aeschylus and remembrances of the Trojan War and the wanderings of Ulysses. And there is always the Bible, especially in its apocalyptic mood, as in Amos and the later chapters of Matthew. In this way the poem's point of departure becomes part of a vast tapestry of human experience, stretching from the beginnings of time.

South Wales Echo attempts in a very striking way to sound out the ultimate realities of death and birth, realities which are mysteries rather than knowable facts. This is perhaps most movingly expressed in the poignant death in childbirth of Mary Anne. Interwoven with this is a sense of protection also, especially at such moments of transition. The priest ministers to the dying woman; the hushed children are entrusted to the care of 'Daddy Howe'; and over all stands the figure of 'blessed Michael the darkangel'. Death and life are part of one thing. The *Verses on the Graves of the Heroes* invoke the unfathomable nature and the ubiquity of death, for they tell us that Arthur's grave is *anoeth*, 'unknown' or a 'mysterious thing' – and indeed though the memory of Arthur remains green in literature and folklore, we do not know where his bones lie.

As with life and death, so light and darkness belong together. Images of fire and light reflect an essential part of the poet's vision. They are the instrument of both destruction and revivification: 'all worlds consumed in everliving fire'. The more one reads, the more one is captivated by the shifts of imagery from the particular to the universal, from the tangible object and visually delineated scene to the cosmic and metaphysical. The 'dark rock and sparkling stone' connect the hard experience of the South Wales coalfield with Ruysbroeck's characterization of the 'white stone' on which is written 'a new name . . . which no man knoweth saving he that receiveth it' (Revelation 2, 17); the stone, of course, is Christ.

South Wales Echo is a deeply Christian poem, but its exploration of the Christian message transcends the limitations of dogmatic Christianity. It taps the springs of universal imagery and symbolism. It is in this context that we have to understand the recurrence of the south and northfacing forms, symbolizing death-in-life and life-in-death. It so happens that the City Gaol, in which the three men await execution, actually faces north, and thus with this simple topographical point the terrifying fate that awaits them is linked with the crucifixion of Christ and the two thieves on Golgotha. Through all the pathos and suffering, through all the alienation of man from his fellow-men, there shines – dimly, perhaps, but it shines nonetheless – the Christian hope and conviction that, in Mother Julian's words, familiar also from *Little Gidding*, though sounding here with a significant variation: 'much will be well/ much manner of thing will be well'.

As the poem reaches its conclusion, it returns to the image of the wind, invoked in the epigraph and in the opening section on the cold autumn night, and transforms it into the basis of a haunting, elemental melody. There is, indeed, throughout the poem a strong rhythm of repeated words and phrases which gives the whole work an effect akin to that of a litany. The aural quality of the words is as striking as the visual range of the poem. Possibly, with appropriate music, *South Wales Echo* would make a magnificent radio production.

From the standpoint of both poetic form and *Weltanschauung*, *South Wales Echo* is unmistakably inspired by the writings of David Jones, especially *The Anathemata* and his later work, and this inspiration is fittingly acknowledged in the dedication. There are similarities also with the poetry of Vernon Watkins, with whom the author shares Maesteg as his birthplace – particularly in the latter's working from a known landscape and well-loved things, animals and birds towards an understanding of their participation in the universal. *South Wales Echo* has, however, its own validity; it is far removed from imitation. It is a remarkably assured work. Its language is exact and amazingly unmannered, though the author garners his harvest of words from far and wide. In a curious and mysterious way the poem emanates *power*. It is like an incantation, but almost infinitely more complex than that word alone suggests. With a single phrase or line it brings profound associations to the surface of consciousness. It has a capacity to move that transcends the limitations of ordinary words.

www.ingramcontent.com/pod-product-compliance
Lightning Source LLC
Chambersburg PA
CBHW081233090426
42738CB00016B/3281